The Garrick Club

A History

For the Benefit of
MARR and Miſs HIPPESLEY,
By a Company of Comedians
From the Theatres in LONDON.

At the Playhouſe in TANKARD STREET
On *Tueſday*, the 21ſt of July.
Will be performed a COMEDY, call'd

The INCONSTANT,
Or, The WAY To WIN HIM.
Young *Mirabel*   by   Mr. GIFFARD,
Captain *Duretête*   by   Mr. LYDDALL,
Biſarre   by   Miſs   HIPPESLEY,

At the End of the Second Act, a *Pantomime Dance*. call'd

The DRUNKEN PEASANT,
Peaſant   by   Mr. YATES,
Clown   by   Mr. VAUGHAM,

To which will be added a New Dramatic *Satire*,
(as it was Performed last Winter at the Theatre in Goodman's Fields,
with great applauſe). call'd

LETHE,
Or, ÆSOP in the SHADES,
Æſop   by   Mr. GIFFARD,

'entrebleu and Sir Roger Rakeit, by Mr. LYDDALL,
Sir Wittling Rattle Mr. MARR, Macboggin Mr. YATES,
Scrape the Attorney Mr. PAGET, Mercury Mrs. DUNSTALL,
Charon Mr. DUNSTALL, Lady Rakeit Mrs YATES,
Mr. Thomas Mr. CROFTS, Miſs Lucy Miſs HIPPESLEY,
That Scene being a Sequel to the VIRGIN UNMASKED,
With an Epilogue, by Miſs HIPPESLEY,
To begin exactly at SEVEN o'Clock.
Tickets to be had, and Places to be taken, at Mr. ROOK'S,
Opposite to the Theatre.

David Garrick's first acknowledged appearance on a playbill at Ipswich on
21 July 1741 under the name of Lyddall.

The Garrick Club
A History

Geoffrey Wansell

For Andrew

with much much love!

First published 2004 by Garrick Club, Garrick Street, London WC2E 9AY
in association with Unicorn Press, 76 Great Suffolk Street, London SE1 0BL

Text © 2004 Geoffrey Wansell
Illustrations © 2004 Garrick Club

www.garrickclub.co.uk

ISBN 0 906290 77 5

Typesetting by Ferdinand Page Design, Surrey
Printed and bound in Great Britain

To my fellow members, past and present

Standing-up Swell. "Morning, Charley! Doing a bit o' Park, eh?"
Swell reclining. "Yaas.—You see I can't do without my weglar Exercise."

NOTE

At the end of certain chapters there are facsimiles of pages from the Reverend R H Barham's distinctive *The Garrick Club: Notices of One Hundred and Thirty-five of its Former Members*, first printed privately in 1896.

On other pages there are cartoons by John Leech who regularly illustrated for *Punch* and became a member of the Garrick Club in 1849.

~ *Contents* ~

~ *List of Plates* ~

List of Plates (contd)

~ *Acknowledgements* ~

F OR ME, writing a history of the Garrick Club is the most
daunting task imaginable, so daunting in fact that I suffered
the most severe writer's block, not to say stage fright, before
I managed to put a single word on paper for this, the fourth history of the Club in its 173 years. The reason was simple enough.
Not only can there hardly be a more intimidating literary task
than to capture the distinctive, unmistakeable charm of the
Garrick for its members, but there is also the frightening prospect
of committing that charm to paper – in a Club that is now, and
always has been, home to so many talented writers.

For months I was convinced that many, many other members were better qualified, and better informed than I was about
the Club and its history, knew better stories and had a finer literary style. But the longer I delayed the more I came to realise
that I was forgetting the Club's tradition of respecting, and looking after, its fellow members, even one who is only in his four-
teenth year. I also realised that to write about the Garrick is to
write about the members, and the members will forgive a fellow
member anything – well, almost anything. With that thought in
my intellectual knapsack, I plucked up the courage to begin.

One other thing encouraged me to embark on the journey: the support of the current Trustees, Anthony Butcher QC, Roger Morgan CBE, Henry McGee and Barry Turner, the current Chairman of the General Committee. They seemed to think I might be able to make something of a fist of it, and so, after much huffing and puffing, not to mention general prevarication, I started, very slowly. But as the time passed I began to enjoy myself, and to understand that any history of the Garrick is but a reflection of the Club itself.

Sit at the centre table on any day and you are not expected to perform miracles, simply to be yourself. That's what three of the previous historians of the Club, Percy Fitzgerald in 1904, Guy Boas in 1948 and Richard Hough in 1982, did so triumphantly. They brought their own particular style to their histories, reflections of their own times and experiences, and I could not have completed this book without their inspiration. Theirs is a great tradition.

The present account owes an enormous amount to the determination of the three most recent chairmen of the General Committee, the late Nunc Willcox, Anthony Butcher QC and Barry Turner. Their support was unwavering, and I deeply appreciated it. The current Chairman of the House Committee, Brian Macarthur, was every bit as supportive, as was the member given the unenviable task of overall editorial consultant, the inimitable Tom Pocock, and the member responsible for its production, Hugh Tempest-Radford, with Sarah Kane copy-editing my text. For the index, I relied on the extraordinary talents of another member, Douglas Mathews. This volume would not exist without them.

But there are other members still whose contributions were equally invaluable. Many of the stories in this history have been passed down through the years from members to their successors, and many of them retold to me. To list every single member who regaled me with a story or reminiscence would be quite impossible, and I hope they will forgive me if I do not mention them all by name, but I owe each and every one of them a great debt. I would just single out two individuals, the former Trustee Sir Donald Sinden and Richard Bebb, who between them seem to have unearthed more details of Garrick history than anyone.

I must also thank one other individual member, however, the Chairman of the Works of Art Committee, John Baskett, for his invaluable help and advice, not to mention his attention to the details of the manuscript. For although this is not a history of the Club's works of art – there are already three fine volumes devoted to those – the pictures are the frieze that brings to life all of the members who went before us, and no one could be more assiduous or thoughtful than John Baskett in reminding us of that legacy.

Among the Club's staff I must also thank Enid Foster, the Club's former Librarian, and Marcus Risdell her successor as well as a non-staff researcher, Samantha Wyndham, whose oral history interviews with so many of our senior members I drew upon, and which will provide a treasure trove for any subsequent historian in the decades to come. I must also thank the Secretary, Martin Harvey, for his forbearance, and his secretary Fiona Murray, for her patience in dealing with my multitude of requests and questions. Indeed, there have been many members of staff who have kindly reminded me of stories about the Club in the past. I hope they too will forgive me for not mentioning each and every one of them individually, but I am enormously grateful to them all.

Not one of the above should be held responsible for my conclusions, however, for those are mine alone. But I hope my fellow members will enjoy the result, and forgive me if they could have done better. I would like to dedicate this history to all members past and present, for they – and the Garrick itself – have transformed my life.

Geoffrey Wansell
London
January 2004

Gordon, Robert, Esq., M.P.

Commonly B—m Gordon.

Gower, Lord Francis Leveson

Afterwards Lord Francis Egerton, author of "Catherine of Cleves," &c. He took the chair at the dinner given by the Club at the Albion Tavern to Charles Kemble on his retiring from the stage.

Graham, Marquess of, M.P.

Eldest son of the Duke of Montrose.

Greaves, Lord

A pauper peer; went to reside on the Continent when he had contracted a discreditable marriage. He was the son of poor Lord Greaves, who cut his throat in consequence of his wife's intriguing with the Duke of Cumberland. I used to meet both father and son at Sir Andrew Barnard's and at Lord William Lennox's. The son was then a Captain in the Guards and was known by the sobriquet of Tommy Tombstones.

Prologue

THE Garrick Club is not haunted – at least not as far as any-one knows – but there are ghosts everywhere nonetheless. The moment that you walk up the stone steps from the street and push open the first pair of double doors, the past seems to sweep over you like a giant breath exhaled by the old, dark, soft stucco-fronted building.

And as you make your way up the second set of stairs, now carpeted in red, the voices of the past seem to whisper to you as the building casts its spell, like a theatre. For a moment it is almost as if you can hear voices, even footsteps, from the past wafting gently across the black and white tiles of the entrance hall. They appear to come from the dark leather chairs that lie under the stairs – the place that more than any other encapsulates all that the Garrick Club stands for.

It is impossible to forget, as the second set of glass doors swing shut behind you, and you find yourself finally in the heart of the building, that this is the hall that welcomed as members Dickens, Trollope and Galsworthy, Henry Irving and Squire Bancroft, Gilbert and Sullivan (though not at the same time), Arthur Ransome, A.A. Milne, Pinero and Maugham, Munnings and Millais from past generations, as well as Olivier, Gielgud and Guinness, Rattigan, Osborne and Amis from more recent ones.

Their laughter, and their tears, seem to hang in the air as you walk up the wide staircase in front of you, past Trollope's letter, David Garrick's chair from Drury Lane, and the chair on which Irving ended his days, towards what is now the Cocktail Bar on the left as you reach the first floor. The vast collection of theatrical portraits hanging beside you stare silently down, acknowledging that you are but the latest in the long line to tread this path.

There may be noise everywhere, as there often can be at lunchtime, or on a busy evening, but there is also a silence, an awareness that you are part of the history that the Garrick represents to each and every one of its 1,100 or so members today, and the ghosts of the members who haunt it still.

But what does that history consist of? What is it that makes the Garrick such a remarkable institution? Why are its members so deeply attached to it, sometimes even more so than to their own families? What is it about the atmosphere and the tradition that makes the Club one of the unique British institutions, and one that continues to flourish to this day?

The Garrick has an exceptional collection of paintings, remarkable holdings of theatrical memorabilia, and an unparalleled library. But what makes it unique are its members – for they, and they alone, make the Club what it was, is and will become. Take the members away and there is no Garrick Club, merely a museum, with a fine library. But put them back and you have an extraordinary institution, as I hope this history will show.

~ I ~

Beginnings

S O HOW did it begin? One thing is certain. David Garrick
had been dead for more than half a century before the
Club that bears his name came anywhere near to existence.
In fact the Garrick Club was the brainchild of an assorted
group of writers, actors, lawyers and landowners, who were
convinced that there should be somewhere in London for actors
to meet new friends. The only difficulty was that actors were
not considered to be entirely respectable in the London of
George IV.

The Garrick came into existence in the shadow of the
Athenaeum (founded 1826) as a meeting place for actors, writers
and painters. That then august institution quickly became, in the
words of another of the Garrick's historians, Guy Boas, 'as hard
to enter as the proverbial eye of the needle'. 'It was not enough
to be an artist, one must be a member of the Royal Academy;
it was not enough to be a writer or a scientist, one must have
written a book, and – further – one must have published it'.

There was certainly room for a club run on the lines of the
Athenaeum, but one that was markedly less formal, and where

the qualifications for membership 'were of a less exacting order', as one founder member put it. The century-older Beefsteak Club specifically excluded actors — although authors, lawyers, painters, politicians, even businessmen were allowed to join. There was space for a club that was not afraid of actors, nor of their friends.

The Garrick was brought into being by a marvellously assorted bunch of men that included the Reverend R.H. Barham, author of *The Ingoldsby Legends*, Francis Mills, 'a frequent contributor to the periodical press' as well as a collector of pictures, James Winston, part-proprietor of the Haymarket Theatre, Samuel Beazley, the architect, James Smith, one of the authors of *Rejected Addresses*, Francis 'Papa' Fladgate, who inherited a 'modest' fortune from his lawyer father and devoted himself to the theatre, and Theodore Hook, editor of *John Bull* magazine and famous as a wit.

Papa Fladgate, sometimes referred to as the 'father of the Garrick', was, in Barham's words, 'one of the most polished gentlemen and good-natured persons I ever met'. Though he did not, in fact, become a member until 1832, his energy and dedication certainly helped to steer the Club through its earliest and most difficult years. With a pronounced stoop in his later years, and renowned for his affability and kindness, as well as a delight in telling stories about his fellow member Kemble and other actors, Fladgate was to remain a member for sixty years — until his death in 1892 at the age of ninety-four.

Fladgate may lay claim to be the 'father' of the Club, but Francis Mills contributed every bit as much to its foundation. No one is quite sure whether it was Mills who invited the Duke of Sussex to become the Club's patron, or whether the duke himself, George III's sixth son, suggested it as a way of meeting journalists and actors rather than courtiers. What is certain is that Mills became one of the original three Trustees of the Club.

A wealthy bachelor, whose brother was MP for Rochester in Kent, Mills was thirty-eight when the idea for the Garrick was first discussed early in 1831, five years after the Athenaeum had come into existence — complete with its formidable frieze, flunkies in tail coats and velvet breeches, and high ambitions. A partner in a timber merchant's in Rotherhithe, and chairman of a life assurance company, he had interests in railways in the United States – and was memorably described by his fellow founder Barham as 'a very good tempered but flighty man'.

An amateur painter, who divided his time between his London house and the family seat, Bisterne Manor, near Ringwood in Hampshire, Mills loved the life of Regency London, but also found time to acquire an apartment in Rome. In the summer of 1831 Mills was in London, wholeheartedly pursuing the idea of a club that was a good deal more 'bohemian' than the Athenaeum.

At a meeting at the Drury Lane Theatre on 17 August 1831 Mills, together with Sir Andrew Barnard, a distinguished general who had been shot through the leg at the storming of San Sebastian and wounded again at Waterloo, the theatre's manager Samuel Arnold, and the architect Samuel Beazley, effectively laid the foundations of the Club. The four men wrote down a list of names of gentlemen 'to be applied to, to join the Garrick Club as original members'. At the next meeting on 21 September they agreed that anyone who had not answered the invitation should be subject to a ballot. The only exception they would countenance was for the Duke of Wellington, victor of Waterloo, and then Prime Minister, but no answer from the duke was ever recorded.

Significantly, none of the early records of the Club reveals precisely why the name Garrick was chosen. Certainly the founding committee were anxious to identify themselves with the theatre – and the name of England's greatest actor of the past century was famous enough, as well as conveying a measure of respectability. The Athenaeum was suitably Olympian, and the recently formed Beefsteak plain enough, but the founders had other, more artistic, aspirations – and Garrick was their way of conveying those hopes.

With the Duke of Sussex, a famous mesmerist and freemason, as patron, Mills and his co-founders agreed that the Club's first President should be the Earl of Mulgrave, a former Governor of Jamaica who became Lord Lieutenant of Ireland ('whence he sent the Club a turtle' – noted Barham later), and he announced its objectives, even before the clubhouse had opened its doors for business. They were for 'actors and men of distinc-

tion to meet on equal terms' and to 'collect a library of reference'
as well as to 'bring back the drama to glory again'.

Mulgrave was succeeded as President by the Duke of
Devonshire but he was little more than 'ornamental', in the words
of the Club's first historian, Percy Fitzgerald, 'for he rarely looked
in'. The Vice-president was Lord Tenterden.

The Garrick was to be a place where, according to
Fitzgerald, 'actors and men of education and refinement might
meet on equal terms … Easy intercourse was to be promoted
between artists and patrons … patrons of the drama and its pro-
fessors, and a rendezvous offered to literary men'. The character
of the Club was to be social, and therefore the Committee 'were
compelled to exercise vigilant care, for it was clear that it would
be better that ten unobjectionable men should be excluded than
one terrible bore should be admitted'.

On more mundane matters Frank Mills, after discussion with
his fellow founders, announced that 'dinners were to be at 5pm and
the bill called at 6.30; and that musical parties were contemplated
on the evenings that the theatres were not open'. 'Conversational
rather than culinary excellence' was the 'object to be aimed at' and
the Club was supposed to be 'inexpensive' – but the joining fee was
fixed at 10 guineas, and the annual subscription at six.

One hundred and seventy gentlemen responded to the original letters of invitation to be members, and the Committee
agreed that the number of members should not exceed 300 in the
first instance. The original membership included two dukes, five
marquesses, six earls and twelve barons, as well as the poet
Samuel Rogers, the dramatist John Poole, the librettist James
Planché, the musician Sir George Smart, as well as the actors
Charles Kemble, William Macready, the comic actor Charles
Mathews and his son Charles James Mathews. There were also
the publishers John Murray and Richard Bentley, who were
quickly joined by the king's printer, William Spottiswoode. There
were even nine MPs, and two Royal Academicians.

Indeed if any one founder member could be said to have
'created' the Garrick it was Mills, who became one of the original
Trustees, only to resign that post within a few weeks 'because of

my frequent absences from England'. He nevertheless served on the Club's General Committee for the first six years of its life, and again in the 1840s.

The idea of a club was one thing, a home for it quite another. After a couple of 'temporary' Committee meetings at the Drury Lane Theatre, and another round the corner at 3 Charles Street, Covent Garden, Mills and his colleagues decided to search for a permanent home. One of London's best-known auctioneers, George Robins, was asked to find premises, and – after a struggle – secured the lease on what had only recently been Probatt's Family Hotel, at 35 King Street, Covent Garden, complete with its furniture and fittings. Robins paid £1,500, and Beazley the architect was given a budget of £500 to convert it.

The building was a snug, old-fashioned house, which had been home to the actor William Lewis before becoming a hotel. Beazley added a smoking room and a bar, as well as smartening up the main dining room. The smaller Coffee Room was for members only. At the top of a flight of stone steps was a gloomy hall, which was eventually to house a bust of Shakespeare, as well as a group of other busts of celebrated actors. On the left was the Strangers' Dining Room, and a long passage led to the Smoking Room – 'which was not', according to a founder member, 'a cheerful apartment by daylight and when empty, but which, at night and full, was thought the most cheerful apartment in Town'.

The Club's first historian, Percy Fitzgerald, writing seven decades later, in 1904, suggested that the foundation of the Garrick marked a 'turning point in the social life and habits' of London. 'It was an attempt to give more correct and official shape to the old jovial tavern intercourse to which all ranks had long been addicted, but which was just beginning to die out.'

The innumerable drinking clubs, with names like the Fly-By-Nights, which met at alehouses were one thing, as were supperhouses like Paddy Green's in Covent Garden – 'where you could eat the succulent chop and well-baked potato, floury and squeezed from its jacket by the deft waiter' – but a club with a defined objective and slightly more formal rules was something altogether different.

The Garrick's foundation was marked on 18 February 1832 with a formal dinner – of 'innumerable courses'. The Club's first patron, the Duke of Sussex, presided, and proposed a toast to the new Club – describing its principal object 'as affording a rallying-point for the lovers of drama'.

At one point during the innumerable courses, a song entitled *The Garrick Club*, with words by James Smith, was sung by the tenor John Braham, who subsequently lost a fortune building what became the St James's Theatre. The line 'To bring back the drama to glory again' was greeted with loud cheers. But the song was followed by a distinctly frivolous glee, composed by Barham, which ran:

> Let poets of superior parts
> Consign to deathless fame
> The larceny of the Knave of Hearts
> Who spoiled his royal dame.
> Alack! My timid muse would quail
> Before such thievish cubs,
> But plumes a joyous wing to hail
> Thy birth – fair Queen of Clubs.

The Garrick announced its arrival as it meant to go on – with a great fanfare. This was not to be a pale imitation of the Athenaeum, to which many actors resorted as a result of the ban at the Beefsteak – the Garrick was to be a place of its own, and proud of it.

Barham may have been a man of the cloth, but he was no respecter of people, particularly not of his fellow members. Indeed he kept a little handwritten notebook about them all: indicating each one's strengths, and foibles. The notes remained private for six decades, half a century after Barham's own death, but in 1896 they were published privately. Barham's notebook reveals a great deal about the characters that made up the Garrick in those early years, and, indeed, about the Club itself. As the editor notes, it provides 'a curious and valuable record of artistic life in London sixty years ago' – and an even more revealing portrait of the Garrick Club.

The tone for the whole book is set by the frontispiece of these 'notices of one hundred and thirty-five former members', which reproduces Barham's handwritten entry for John Forster, one of the original members. His tiny handwriting reads: 'A low scribbler, without an atom of talent and totally unused to the society of gentlemen. He narrowly escaped expulsion, from publishing an account of a dinner at the Garrick in a newspaper to which he was a reporter. The Committee wrote him a letter on the occasion expressive of their disgust, which would have caused any other man to retire'.

But the note doesn't end there. Indeed it goes on: 'About a year after he got beastly drunk at the anniversary Club dinner, and was sick in Sergeant Talfourd's pocket. Tom Duncombe got drunk at the same time, but behaved so different that Poole observed one was the real gentleman drunk, the other the "spewrious" gentleman drunk. He subsequently became a sort of toady to Sergeant Talfourd and Macready, and wrote theatrical criticisms for the Examiner'. In fact Forster, who was later to become Dickens's biographer and close friend, was later defended by the Garrick's original historian, Percy Fitzgerald, who insisted: 'a truer friend and a kinder heart it was impossible to conceive', though he went on to admit that he 'was always treading, or trampling, on people's corns'.

Forster was not the only member to feel the rough side of Barham's pen. The barrister John Adolphus didn't fare much better. 'He was a man full of anecdote', Barham notes, 'but occasionally very rude, which made him, though a very eloquent, also a very unpopular member at the Bar, and unquestionably prevented his rising to the highest rank in his profession'. A defender of doubtful cases at the Old Bailey, he also had literary pretensions, having written a 'ponderous' life of George III.

The baronet Sir Wyndham Anstruther, who had once been a 'player on the Margate stage' is dismissed as 'a regular scamp. Having spent every shilling he was worth while Captain

Anstruther, he was at dinner on bread and cheese with a half pint of porter at the Brown Bear, a flash house in Bow Street, when he saw in the paper the sudden death of his cousin, the young baronet, who was killed by some accident while a boy at Eton. This event gave him a baronetcy and an entailed estate of several thousands a year, all of which that he could touch he dissipated in less than two years'. Barham was horrified by his behaviour and went on: 'having joined with Tom Duncombe and Horace Cleggat, etc, in raising £40,000 by accommodation bill, received the money and ran away to France with it, leaving his friends subject to all the liabilities. He was afterwards outlawed, and his name struck off the list of the Club by the Committee'.

The founding members of the Committee, however, weren't a great deal more respectable. Barham describes his fellow Committee man, theatre owner Samuel Arnold, for example, as: 'one of the leading members of the Beef Steak Club, where he was called the Bishop and used to say a mock (but not profane) grace in a large white mitre. The sobriquet by which he was generally known was "Sambo". Latterly he took to drinking spirits and water till he became quite a sot'. Things got so bad that Arnold resigned from the Club, and the Committee, in 1835 due to 'the deranged state of his affairs' and went to live in Boulogne.

But some of the early members of the Committee fared better. Barham was a particular supporter, for example, of the architect of the King Street building, Samuel Beazley, whom he described as 'one of the most good humoured, lively companions in the world'. He did, however, point out that his marriages were distinctly unhappy. 'From his first wife he was separated by a Scotch divorce ... He afterwards ran away with Miss Coust, natural daughter of the Chairman of the Middlesex Sessions, who in turn ran away from him to her father and procured a divorce on the grounds of impotency'.

Barham also recorded one of the earliest bursts of public temper exhibited by a member of the Club. It would certainly not be the last. In February 1833, a year after the grand inaugural dinner, the MP Thomas Duncombe, one of the founder members, was backstage at Drury Lane one evening when the proprietor of the Sunday newspaper *The Age*, a Mr Westmacott, came up to him and asked him how he was. Duncombe was incensed. 'I am surprised, sir', he snapped, 'that you should think of addressing me when you are abusing me constantly in your paper, and I desire that when you do speak to me you will take off your hat'. At that moment he snatched Westmacott's hat from his head and threw it to the ground. Then, as the newspaper man took off his gloves, Duncombe hit him, twice, in the face – and only stopped when the onlookers grabbed him.

There was talk of a duel, and 'information' was lodged at the magistrates' court in Bow Street – it was still seven years before the arrival of Sir Robert Peel's metropolitan police. But in the end apologies were made, and the matter passed. Nevertheless Barham does record, with a distinctly mischievous tone, that 'on calling at the Garrick the next morning Duncombe was publicly thanked by Mathews, Planché, and some others for having thrashed his opponent'.

Barham's descriptions of his fellow founder members shine from the page of his notebook to this day. Charles Ellis, for example, was, 'A half made attorney, who was constantly drunk and as constantly quarrelsome, though very good natured during his few intervals of sobriety'. The proprietor and editor of the *Sunday Times*, Thomas Gaspey, was 'a low-bred vulgar man', while the barrister Frederick Osborne was 'a very disagreeable, overbearing, rude man, and generally cut on the Circuit'.

But Barham is excellent on the character of the two men who – after the Club's energetic founder Frank Mills – did more than any others to make the Garrick the place it was to become. The two were the comic actor Charles Mathews, and the self-made businessman John Durrant. It was Mathews and Durrant who gave the Club the foundations of its collection of theatrical paintings and portraits – now acknowledged as one of the finest in the world. Yet, as ever, the Garrick – its Committee and its members – acted idiosyncratically.

THE GARRICK CLUB

Beazley, Samuel, Esq.

The architect ; one of the most good-humoured,
lively companions in the world. He was the
only bearable punster I ever knew, except
Peake. Both his marriages were unfortunate.
From his first wife he was separated by a
Scotch divorce, though having been married in
England some doubts were entertained as to
the legality of it. He afterwards ran away
with Miss Coust, natural daughter of the
Chairman of the Middlesex Sessions, who in
her turn ran away from him to her father,
and procured a divorce on the ground of impotency. She afterwards ran away again from
her father with young Arnold, son to Sam
Arnold, before mentioned, and married him. I
met her once with Beazley at Hawes's, when
I never saw a man more attentive to his wife
than he was, but the lady seemed to receive
it all most ungraciously. This was about
three years before their separation, which
took place circiter 1833. Beazley was one
of those who went up in the Royal Balloon
in 1837.

10

$\sim 2 \sim$

Books and Paintings

O ONE was a more valuable founder member of the Garrick than the stockbroker John Rowland Durrant. This 'kindly, upright man', to use Barham's phrase, who had made himself a fortune by selling parcels of stock during the Napoleonic Wars was a passionately keen amateur actor with a private box at Drury Lane, was given all manner of responsibilities by the Committee.

It was Durrant who, in the autumn of 1831, negotiated the details of the lease on Probatt's Hotel in King Street with Probatt himself. He reported to the Committee on 21 October that the hotel's owner 'had agreed to take £2,000 instead of £2,400 – the sum he had first asked'. The final sum needed turned out to be £2,710, after legal expenses, and Durrant himself offered to lend the money – 'in case the Bankers should refuse to advance the sum' – to be repaid as the subscriptions came in. In the event, the bankers obliged.

It was another founder member, the barrister John Adolphus, who inspired the Garrick to start its library, proposing that every member present the Club with 'his duplicate dramatic books'. Indeed when the formal rules of the Club eventually came to be written, 'the formation of a theatrical library' became one of its objects – though in the first years it was the formation of a collection of paintings that was the Garrick's first priority.

The Club had already been given David Garrick's candlesticks – which sat on the mantelpiece in King Street, and had been lent a number of paintings by the founder members, particularly by the comedian Charles Mathews, who had gathered an extraordinary collection of theatrical works in the thirty years since he had become a star in 1803.

In July 1835, the Garrick again called on John Durrant's negotiating skills, and his generosity, to 'make enquiries relating to the late Mr C Mathews Gallery of the Portraits, and the sum they can be purchased for'.

Tall and skinny, Mathews was a comic actor with a mouth that 'moved all over his face', according to one contemporary. Born in Richmond in 1776, the son of a bookseller, he had persuaded his father to let him go onto the stage as a teenager, and had spent ten years acting in small parts in Dublin, Swansea and York at a miserable salary. Then in 1803, at the age of twenty-seven, Mathews made his breakthrough with a performance at the Haymarket Theatre in London. He had found a way of bringing his extraordinary ability as a mimic, and sometime ventriloquist, to bear on the audience, and for three decades he could do almost no wrong. Shortly after the English victory at Waterloo Mathews initiated a series of what were called 'At Homes' at Drury Lane, one-man theatrical readings in which he played a number of characters. They were a triumph.

He celebrated his success by sending his son Charles to Eton, and starting a collection of paintings. Not that he thought he could do it alone. He was too busy with his career for that, and so he sought the help of the artist Samuel De Wilde, who was twenty-five years his senior. At the time De Wilde was looking for patronage, and Mathews was the ideal client, so good, in fact, that the two men became close friends. It was the perfect partnership. Mathews wanted to acquire theatrical pictures, drawings and prints, De Wilde was not only skilled in painting and drawing actors and actresses himself, but was also well connected enough to act as Mathews's agent. That was not all, however. No fewer than 185 works in Mathews's eventual collection were by De Wilde himself.

In 1819 Mathews moved into Ivy Cottage on the edge of Kenwood on the borders of Highgate and Hampstead in north London, and shortly afterwards his son – who had gone on to train as an architect under Augustus Welby Pugin – designed a picture gallery and small Gothick library as an extension to his father's new house. But then, quite suddenly, everything started to go wrong for Mathews. In the late 1820s he lost all his money in a speculation, not uncommon in the period but desperate nonetheless, and was forced to sell his beloved Ivy Cottage, before moving to more modest accommodation. Worse still, he was also forced to sell his collection of by now almost 400 paintings, prints and drawings of theatrical subjects.

The only trouble was that Mathews couldn't find a buyer. In desperation he tried putting the collection on show in the Queen's Bazaar in Oxford Street, but that failed miserably. Part of the problem was the price. Mathews was not asking what he thought they were worth – only what he had paid for them. But that was still more than £3,000: no small sum in 1830.

Still trying to keep his creditors at bay, Mathews lent a small part of his collection to the newly formed Garrick Club, of which he was a founder member. Indeed they were some of the first things hung on the walls of the new Club building in King Street. He also made discreet enquiries of his fellow members. Might the Club be prepared to purchase them from him? But it was to no avail. For a period the Committee maintained a studied silence – even though he was offering Johan Zoffany's famous painting *The Clandestine Marriage* at just £50, and his *Macbeth* at £30. But in 1833 they made it clear that they were not prepared to meet Mathews's asking price. The tall, spindly actor was heartbroken, and within two years he was dead, at the age of fifty-nine.

In July 1835, shortly after Mathews's death, the indefatigable, and ever reliable Durrant was instructed by the Committee to enquire about the Mathews Collection. A month later he reported that the Club had 'refusal ... at one thousand pounds' – which experts have since estimated was between five and ten per cent of its value. Mathews's widow and son had no alternative but to accept. A General Meeting of the Club took place on the afternoon of Friday 14 August 1835 'to take into consideration a proposal for purchasing the collection of pictures and drawings formed by the late Charles Mathews'. Forty-seven members of the Garrick turned up for the meeting, and, after an hour's deliberation, duly instructed the Committee to buy the collection.

But they did not intend to pay for the pictures themselves. They intended to borrow the money – and the man they intended to borrow it from was, of course, John Rowland Durrant, who agreed without a moment's hesitation. At a single stroke the Garrick had acquired the foundation of what was to become the greatest collection of theatrical pictures in the world – without spending a penny of its own money.

Durrant's generosity to the Garrick did not end there. Over the next fifteen years Durrant regularly lent the Committee money to keep the Club afloat. There was £300 in 1838, £200 in 1840, 1841, 1843 and 1844 and £250 in 1845 – a total of £1,550 in all. And all the while the debt of £1,000 for the Mathews Collection was still outstanding. In September 1852 Durrant decided to write off the £1,000 loan, refusing even to accept the five per cent interest that he had been guaranteed, and communicated his decision to the Club early in 1853. In April the Committee wrote to express its gratitude. 'We need scarcely to assure you', they wrote, 'that so long as the Collection of Pictures by which you enabled us to impress its happiest character on our association shall endure; your munificence will be fondly cherished'.

Just three months later, in July 1853, the ever generous Durrant was dead. The gift of the Mathews Collection had been his last act of munificence – an act for which successive members owe him an enormous debt of gratitude. In recognition of his extraordinary contribution it was agreed that a small brass plaque should be placed in the entrance hall. It was to read: 'The paintings and drawings collected by the late Charles Mathews were presented to the Garrick Club by John Rowland Durrant Esq 1852'. The plaque, high up on the left-hand side of the entrance stairs, above the clock, as one enters the building remains there today. It is a barely adequate tribute to the Club's first great benefactor.

The Mathews Collection of some 235 items represents almost a quarter of the Club's current collection of paintings, drawings, sculpture and prints – and includes many of its single most famous pictures, including Zoffany's *The Clandestine Marriage* and *Macbeth*, both of which hang in the Coffee Room still. *The Clandestine Marriage*, which is currently displayed above the Coffee Room's mantelpiece near the entrance, but may move in a rehanging of the pictures in the next few years, is the Club's best-known, and best-loved, painting. The play itself was written by David Garrick, then the manager of Drury Lane and George Coleman, manager of Covent Garden, just round the corner, and hinges on a classic comic situation in which Lord Ogelby mistakes a young woman's confidences for an amorous approach.

As so often in the history of the Garrick, however, what seems respectable on the surface turns out to be rather less so on careful inspection. The actress playing the young woman in Zoffany's painting is none other than Sophia Baddeley, whose beauty – and sexual promiscuity – was famous on the eighteenth-century stage. Even worse, her husband, who is shown playing the Swiss valet, and appears in the background of the picture, often acted as her pimp.

For a time in the eighteenth century Zoffany was effectively David Garrick's in-house artist. He had arrived in England from Germany in 1760, but found life as an artist so hard that he was barely able to scrape a living. Times were so hard, in fact, that his wife left him. It was while he was eking out a living working as an assistant in Benjamin Wilson's studio that Garrick discovered him. Garrick saw in the young Zoffany someone who could paint him in various plays, paintings that could then be engraved in mezzo-tint, and used to produce promotional material for his perform-ances. The actor became Zoffany's patron – and remained so for a decade, until the painter was introduced to George III. From that moment on Zoffany gradually slipped out of Garrick's life, enticed, no doubt, by the attractions of life at court, where he and the king probably spoke to each other in German.

Several portraits of Garrick adorn the walls of the Club now, the most famous of which is Zoffany's small head, a little under four feet by three feet, which hangs in the middle of the window wall in the Coffee Room. An unfinished section of what was probably to have been a larger work, it was, some believe, given to the Club by none other than its greatest single benefactor – John Durrant – on his own account. Another great work by Zoffany, also in the Coffee Room, shows Garrick as Macbeth and Hannah Pritchard as Lady Macbeth. The scene is from Act Two, when Macbeth, struggling with guilt and with his hands still bloodstained, can't make himself plant the two daggers on the sleeping grooms. Lady Macbeth snaps: 'Infirm of purpose!/Give me the daggers'.

Garrick had played Macbeth for the first time at Drury Lane on 7 January 1744, but not with Hannah Pritchard. She did not join him to play Lady Macbeth until four years later, but their joint performance became one of the great partnerships of the London stage for the next twenty years, and Zoffany celebrated their triumph in this painting. Her last performance came in 1768, when she retired. She died a few months later. The odd thing was that throughout her twenty years of playing the role she never knew, nor even, by all accounts, enquired as to how the play ended. Another was that she was considerably taller than Garrick, who stood just five feet four, while she was six feet. Garrick almost certainly instructed Zoffany not to paint the long feather that she always wore in her hat for the performance – to even things up a little. Zoffany took his revenge by painting Garrick's built-up shoes.

Yet another great Zoffany, which likewise hangs in the Coffee Room today, also arrived as part of the Mathews Collection. Garrick and Susanna Cibber appear as Jaffeir and Belvedira in the now all-but-forgotten play *Venice Preserv'd* by Thomas Otway. Once again Garrick is the tragic hero, poised with a knife raised, while Cibber kneels at his feet in supplication.

Zoffany probably completed the painting early in 1763, but, as usual, indulged his artistic licence – the actual scene takes place in the senate, and certainly not at the edge of the Grand Canal with the Church of the Salute in the distance.

Between them Charles Mathews and John Durrant established the nucleus of the Garrick's significant collection of British theatrical works of art, which now amounts to almost 1,000 paintings and drawings, as well as fifty-six pieces of sculpture. The collection's particular strength lies in works of art from the years 1760 to 1830, a period that has since become known as the 'golden age of theatrical portraiture'. Almost all such works came from Mathews, and so if Frank Mills is owed the greatest credit as the founder member who did more than anyone else to get the Garrick started, it is Mathews who deserves acclaim for creating the finest part of its collection of paintings.

Not that Mathews was entirely alone. Two other painters, David Roberts and Clarkson Stanfield, also made their contributions. Roberts, the son of a shoemaker and born just outside Edinburgh, became a house painter and then a scenery painter, working originally in Scotland, progressing through the north of England and ending up at Drury Lane. His friend Clarkson Stanfield, a former collier who had been press-ganged into the Royal Navy in 1812, only to return and devote himself to painting, put Roberts up for membership of the Club in 1835. Together they set about painting large pictures to decorate the Smoking Room of the original premises in King Street. One of Roberts's greatest works, *View of the Temple of the Sun at Baalbec*, continues to play the role it was originally devised for, and covers the entire end wall of the Irving Room today. A large painting by Roberts's great friend Stanfield, *A Dutch Blazer Coming Out of Monnickendam, Zuyder Zee*, still adorns the Club's walls to this day.

But more than anyone else, it was the unsung John Durrant who not only ensured the survival of the Garrick from its infancy through the first twenty-five years of its life, but also gave it its unrivalled picture collection. Sadly, despite the wealth of portraits of so many other members of the period, no portrait exists of

Durrant himself (nor indeed of Mills). There is only the small plaque in the entrance hall to commemorate his extraordinary contribution to the Club.

First Feuds

N O ONE can explain precisely how or why it happened. Perhaps it was the food, or the wine cellar that was gradually established as the Garrick began to prosper during the 1830s and 1840s, but most likely it was the very atmosphere of the Club. One thing is clear, however – within a matter of years the Garrick had become a London institution.

Iconoclastic, tolerant, good-natured, welcoming, all are apt descriptions of the Club then, as now, bringing the place, even in its comparatively cramped headquarters in King Street, a unique sense of atmosphere and bonhomie. Within the space of two decades the Garrick had established itself as one of the most remarkable facets of early Victorian London. As the Club's second historian, Guy Boas, put it: 'The Garrick, like the Athenaeum, was hardly born before it became an institution'.

The novelists William Makepeace Thackeray and Captain Frederick Marryat had become members in the first years, to be joined by politicians like Lord John Russell, a future Foreign Secretary under Palmerston, William Cavendish, the 7th Duke of Devonshire, Chancellor of both Cambridge and the newly founded London University, as well as MP for Cambridge University.

Another early member was William Lamb MP, later to become Lord Melbourne, and Prime Minister, who was nevertheless best known for his wife, Lady Caroline Lamb, notorious for her passion for Byron. 'Throughout all this exhibition', comments Percy Fitzgerald, 'Mr Lamb showed himself the most indulgent and tolerant of husbands, trying to believe and hope for the best, soothing and encouraging his erratic spouse'.

There were also fashionable figures like the painter and man-about-town the Count d'Orsay, whom Mathews described as the 'beau ideal of manly dignity and grace', who helped set the style for metropolitan London. When the Count painted the Duke of Wellington's portrait in the first year of the Club's existence, the duke declared: 'Thank God, at last I have been painted like a gentleman'.

Not all the members were so exalted, however, though they brought their own individual qualities to the Club. Theodore Hook, for example, one of the founders, and editor of *John Bull* magazine, loved practical jokes. Remembered by many as the 'buoyant and irresistible Theodore Hook', he was, at least according to Fitzgerald, 'the most spontaneous and original of all our wits', and famous for making up songs at the piano about everyone present. On one notable occasion Hook jammed Berners Street, just north of Soho, with an extraordinary crowd – from the Duke of Gloucester and the Lord Mayor of London to chimney sweeps and errand boys – all tempted to turn up by 4,000 letters sent out by Hook asking them to besiege the house of a certain Mrs Tottenham, whom Hook disliked.

Hook liked to entertain his fellow members after dinner with extempore poems, usually about a contemporary political or literary event, or something that had happened recently in the Club. He once called the publisher John Murray 'the Hind-Quarterly reviewer' because he had condemned a book in the Club that he had only looked at the spine of, though never actually read. Not that Murray, the publisher who had paid Byron £2,000 for his works, deserved such a hard time. Not only was he a founder member of the Club but he had also ensured that the works of Jane Austen and Thomas Crabbe reached the reading public.

Among the early actor members, arguably the most distinguished was the versatile Charles Kemble, whose wide-set eyes and open face shine from two portraits by Henry Briggs, both of which still hang in the Club. Credited with 'a greater range than any actor except Garrick', his Hamlet was hailed by one critic – who 'never imagined there could be so much charm in words as mere sounds'. Born in South Wales in 1775 into an acting dynasty – two brothers and two sisters were also actors – Kemble became the ultimate 'dependable' actor, playing a vast range of parts, and turning himself into a stalwart of the London theatre in the first three decades of the nineteenth century. William Macready memorably called him 'a first-rate actor in second-rate parts'. An original member of the Garrick, his health had begun to fail around the time the Club was founded, and he became Examiner of Plays for the Lord Chamberlain in 1836. The years before his death in 1854, at the remarkable age of seventy-nine, were spent as a 'venerated relic' in the Club.

Another of the Club's more idiosyncratic members was the distinctly strange Charles Reade, who was memorably described as 'a slightly cantankerous philanthropist' by Boas, and who, besides writing stories, also 'developed a mania for trading in violins'. A keen cardplayer, Reade once took offence at being called 'Old Cockeywax' by a fellow player, and stormed out. The next day the two players met, and Reade explained that he strongly objected to the name. 'But', said his fellow member, 'you are mistaken. I never called you "old Cockeywax" but "old Cockeylorum" '. Reade beamed, saying that 'makes all the difference ... we can shake hands'.

Other enthusiastic founder members included Sir George Smart, organist at the Chapel Royal and 'the King's organist', who used to travel to Vienna to consult with Beethoven on the tempi of his symphonies, Sergeant Talfourd, MP for Reading, who was responsible for the 1842 Copyright Act, and Samuel Rogers, the poet who turned down the offer to become Poet Laureate and of whom it was said 'no man toiled harder to produce less'.

But the most memorable of the founder members was undoubtedly the Reverend Richard Barham, who was always said to be the source for his fellow member Charles Dickens's character Traddles in *David Copperfield*. Not only was he the author of the definitive work on the personalities of his fellow founder members (see chapter 1), but he was also held in the very highest esteem by each and every one of them. Percy Fitzgerald called him 'a singular compound of Hyde and Jekyll', one moment a decorous clergyman, who ended up as a divinity lecturer, and at the next a bohemian and 'haunter of the Garrick'.

Educated at St Paul's School and Brasenose College, Oxford, Barham had been crippled as a result of an accident during his schooldays, which left him with a ruined right arm. But the disability never detracted from his sense of fun. Author of *The Ingoldsby Legends*, which he wrote at the request of a fellow member, he was also famous for his humorous verse.

'Racy, dignified, shrewd, and kind-hearted', in the words of Boas, Barham acted as Chairman of the Committee for several years, and usually answered complaints from his fellow members in verse. When the aptly named surgeon Michael Blood, for example, objected to the charge of sixpence extra for food ordered between four o'clock and nine, Barham replied:

> Dear Sir, the Committee direct me to say
> That the bill's quite correct which was sent you today;
> It was not eight o'clock when you sat down to dine,
> And we charge for the table from four until nine.
> They've not the least wish your remonstrance to stifle,
> But you're wrong – and they'll thank you to pay them
>   this trifle

But it is Barham's notebook about fellow members that will be his lasting legacy, for it so precisely captured the spirit of cheerful iconoclasm that was to become the Garrick's trademark.

There was Mr Beloe, a member of the Committee, who was assisted in drying his gunpowder, before going off to shoot pheasant with a dentist, by what Barham dubbed 'an officious servant' who succeeded only in blowing up the said Mr Beloe. There was Viscount Allen, forever called 'cantankerous Allen' by Barham, and Lord de Roos, who, though 'very popular', was also 'convicted of cheating at whist and marking the cards'.

There was also the barrister Joseph Douglas, who was 'a member of the Committee and a very gentlemanly man, but fond of his bottle, who used to sing Northern songs, after a fashion'. Douglas died a sad death. Living alone in chambers in the Temple on Christmas Eve, he fell down, hit his head and died from loss of blood. His neighbours downstairs heard him staggering and groaning, but 'as he was in his usual state' took no notice.

Then there was Sir Harry Goodriche, Bart, a leading light of the Quorn Hunt, who died leaving a fortune of £20,000 – 'but never paid his subscription', as well as Lord Greaves 'the pauper peer' who went to live 'on the Continent when he had contracted a discreditable marriage'. The habit ran in the family. Greaves's father 'cut his throat in consequence of his wife's intriguing with the Duke of Cumberland'.

Not that everything was always rosy behind the Garrick's doors in King Street, Covent Garden: far from it. Indeed, critics of the Club and all it stood for were never far away. One newspaper report in 1838, for example, condemned the place roundly. 'Let anyone go past the concern in King Street, and look at the dirty, greasy-haired literary exquisites lolling at the Club window with their fingers unconsciously wandering into their ears and noses ... let him look closer, and if he examines the breast of the literary dandy, he will see a coarse black shirt, not quite concealed by the sham front, which he washes out in his own garret every two days, and puts on by way of concealing the dinginess under his calico'. The report ended, 'The only thing that keeps the affair afloat is that some of the respectable members, who do pay their subscriptions, make up for the defalcations of the shabby gang of members who do not'.

Criticism was not restricted to outsiders, however. Alfred Bunn, who was manager of both Drury Lane and Covent Garden from 1833 to 1848, for example, took a particular dislike to the

Garrick and all it stood for — so strong a dislike, in fact, that not long after the Club opened he included an attack on it in his book *The Stage Both Before and Behind the Curtain*. The attack was all the more embarrassing because his publisher was Richard Bentley, a founder member. Bentley was so distressed by the manuscript that he dissociated himself from it in a foreword, explaining: 'the opinions expressed are those of the Author ... and are adopted, as he conceives, on misinformation'.

In Bunn's opinion the Garrick was 'one of the most detrimental institutions to the best interests of the drama, and the well being of the two patent theatres [Drury Lane and Covent Garden], that was ever established'. The reason, according to Bunn, was that the original object of bringing together players and patrons had been 'lost sight of' because the Club had stopped being 'select'. 'The Club, shorn of its proper supporters', he insisted, 'has degenerated into some sort of Junior Law Club. At its tables congregate some of the soi-disant critics, who gather together what little dramatic intelligence they deal in from the gabble and hoaxing of waggish bystanders, whose notions of actors' performances are usually derived from what they have heard a self-satisfied actor say of himself'.

Bunn didn't stop there, adding: 'Not a domestic calamity amongst the many to which theatrical life is subject but it is known here the moment it happens, and is discussed with mysterious avidity. The daily object of its visitors is to listen to the cancans of the green room ... to retail the jokes of some author over the bottle ... to lure brother-members to the fascination of the dinner table instead of tempting them to the enjoyment of a private box'.

The portly Bunn, who was said by one member to possess 'a hooked nose, his coat covered with frog-braiding, his fingers with splendid rings, and his neck encircled with a jewelled chain', condemned the Garrick for providing 'many worthy people, who prefer not to give their address, the opportunity of dating and receiving letters that have all the appearance of coming from, and going to, a very important place'. He also didn't care for the fact that the members were afforded 'coals and candles gratis' or 'the use of pens, ink and paper', not to mention newspapers. 'All this may be exceedingly pleasant,' he concluded fiercely, 'but it has no connection whatever with the advancement of the drama; on the contrary, it leads to its degradation'. The bitterness of Bunn's attack may just have had something to do with the fact that he had failed to become a member himself, in spite of a letter of support from the Duke of Beaufort.

But Bunn was not alone in his criticism of the Garrick. One or two of the founder members shared his views, not least the actor William Macready, who referred to it in his diary on 5 October 1833 as 'really a blackguard place'; adding three years later, on 9 December 1836: 'Dined at the Garrick Club, where the principal conversation is eating, drinking, or the American presidency. It is really a disgusting place'. Not long afterwards he confessed in his diary that he was afraid that he 'might get into a heat with some of the low and vulgar frequenters of the place'.

Macready, however, reserved his greatest ire for Alfred Bunn, whom he simply couldn't stand. The two had fallen out repeatedly over the years – and in 1836 had come to blows. Bunn had wanted Macready to perform just three acts of Shakespeare's *Richard III* – to leave room for two other elements on the bill. Macready was outraged, so angry in fact that he marched into Bunn's rooms at Drury Lane and knocked him down, closing one of his eyes, spraining his ankle, and leaving – in Bunn's own words – 'my person plentifully soiled with blood, lamp-oil, and ink, the table upset and Richard the Third holding me down'. Macready did not deny the attack – only explaining in his own diary that Bunn had screamed 'Murder! Murder!' – and that, as a result, 'several persons came into the room'.

In the wake of the attack Bunn sued Macready and was awarded £150 in damages, confirming for ever the two men's enmity. And when three of Bunn's closest friends were elected to the Garrick in December 1837, Macready could stand it no more – and left. 'This puts the seal upon the door', he wrote in his diary. 'I will not have anything more to do with it'. But the enmity between Bunn and Macready in the Garrick's early years was a trifle compared to the dispute between Thackeray and Dickens – a dispute that cast a shadow over the Club for more than a decade.

~4~

Thackeray and Dickens

*I*F DURING its first two decades Charles Dickens was the Club's greatest star among the reading public, he was challenged for the title among the members by William Makepeace Thackeray. Dickens was a member of the Garrick on sufferance, never caring all that much for its idiosyncrasies. Thackeray, on the other hand, thought of it as his 'very home', as one member put it at the time. He didn't just pop in from time to time to read the paper, or write a letter, he was a stalwart from the moment he became a member in 1833 until his death, and called it, at one Club dinner, 'the dearest place in the world'.

Fitzgerald, the Garrick's first official historian, was in no doubt whom the members cared for: it was Thackeray. He described his as 'the choicest spirit of the Club, who was during his time the Club itself – its centre, its soul, its cynosure'. The Club was a 'sort of whetting stone for his wit' and kept 'his humours bright, keen and polished'. At one stage Thackeray's bust used to stand opposite Charles Kemble's at the top of the main stairs. 'For everyone who mounts the stair', Fitzgerald wrote, 'it seems to revive the memory of the great writer' who 'looks benevolently on his co-mates'.

Thackeray was not a founder member, however. He was elected barely a year after the Club's foundation, on 22 June 1833. A 'slim young man, rather taciturn, and not displaying any particular love or talent for literature', according to one of the founder members, Planché, he was twenty-two, and still a journalist. At the time, Planché remembered later, he preferred drawing. 'He often sat by my side while I was reading, covering any scrap of paper with amusing caricatures.'

The son of a collector for the East India Company who died when his son was aged three, Thackeray was born in Calcutta in 1811, but sent home to England after his father's death. He went to Charterhouse School, where he was miserable, and Trinity College, Cambridge, which he left in 1830 without taking his degree. By that time he had also contrived to squander part of his inheritance, by gambling. When Macready ran into him in the spring of 1836, Thackeray confessed that he had 'spent all his fortune' and was now 'about to settle in Paris, I believe, as an artist'. The French expedition was not destined to last, even though he married Isabella Shaw while he was there. He worked as a journalist to support his new family.

The Thackerays returned to London in 1837, where his first child, Anne, was born later that year. A second daughter, born in 1839, did not live long, and after the birth of their third, Harriet, Isabella suffered a mental breakdown. Still supporting himself as a journalist, writing for *The Times* among other newspapers, Thackeray placed her in the care of a French doctor in Paris, and sent his children to live with her.

Another later writer member, Anthony Trollope, who joined in 1862, described Thackeray as 'a widower to the end of his days', even though his wife did not die until 1892. The author turned to the Garrick 'not as a luxury but as an anodyne', as another member once put it. Though he was a member of many other clubs – including the Athenaeum – 'on his own testimony the Garrick did more to assuage the heartache of that proud, lonely, supersensitive figure than any other refuge'.

Thackeray's membership of the Club was to be forever coloured, and some said saddened, by the arrival of another author, just a year younger than he was, and elected in 1837, at the age of twenty-five. The young Charles Dickens was elected shortly after his *Pickwick Papers*, which had been appearing in weekly parts, became a literary sensation – though he hadn't been all that enthusiastic about the idea of joining the Club.

The son of an admiralty clerk imprisoned for debt, Dickens was born in Chatham in Kent in 1811, but found himself consigned to a blacking factory at the age of twelve – events that were to inhabit almost every one of his novels. He started work as an office boy, studied shorthand, and eventually worked his way to becoming a parliamentary reporter for the *Morning Chronicle*. A year before his election to the Garrick he had published a collection of his articles for newspapers about contemporary life called *Sketches by Boz*, which attracted considerable attention.

In April 1836 the first of what were to become twenty monthly instalments of *The Posthumous Papers of the Pickwick Club* was published. It was to appear in book form the following year, and – buoyed up by what he later called its 'immense popularity' – Dickens decided to marry the young Catherine Hogarth, then still a minor. Less than a year later *Oliver Twist* began to appear in monthly instalments in *Bentley's Miscellany*, a new periodical that Dickens had been invited to edit by Richard Bentley, a founder member of the Garrick. It was to be followed by *Nicholas Nickleby*. In fact Dickens was pressed to join the Garrick Club by Bentley, though he was not keen on the idea. 'I have consented to the honour', he wrote to a friend, 'and am to be proposed forthwith – by whom I do not know'.

In fact Dickens was never a Garrick enthusiast in the way that Thackeray was. In one of his *Sketches by Boz*, published before he became a member, for example, he describes certain 'theatrical young gentlemen as imagining that to be a member of the Garrick Club, and see so many actors in their plain clothes, must be one of the highest gratifications that the world can bestow'.

By the time that Thackeray's own success as an author had been cemented in 1848 with the publication of *Vanity Fair*, the two men had been stalking around each other like gaming cocks in the Club for years. The sensitive, rather sad Thackeray always seemed uncomfortable in the presence of the brasher, more tempestuous Dickens. 'I never saw Thackeray and Dickens engaged in regular conversation', recalled one member later. 'If either of them entered a room when the other and only one or two more, perhaps, were its occupants, he seemed to have come in to look for something he had mislaid, and, if he did not make an abrupt exit, stayed only to bury himself in a newspaper, or in forty winks'.

Thin-faced, tall, and forever batting aside some imagined slight, Dickens never seemed entirely comfortable in the Club, not least perhaps because of Thackeray being so obviously 'ruler of the roost' there, as Percy Fitzgerald put it in his history. 'It was foolish of the younger man, 'he wrote, 'one of the light, "freelances of the Press", to think of disputing such a supremacy'. But dispute it he did.

Dickens didn't care for Thackeray, regardless of the success of *Vanity Fair*, and the feeling was mutual. Thackeray even told his daughter in a letter that 'there is not room for us both up the same tree'; which led, as Fitzgerald later sadly acknowledged, to 'a certain acidity in their relations'. But the acidity didn't stop with the two principals, it communicated itself to their friends – with disastrous results.

In fact Dickens resigned from the Club for the first time in December 1849, though he gave no reason. Five years later he was back again, reinstated after encouragement from his friends, with the support of more than fifty members and the agreement of the Committee – whom he thanked in a letter 'for their cordial welcome'. He immediately accepted their invitation to chair the Club's annual dinner to celebrate Shakespeare's birthday. One member who was there that evening commented: 'Dickens was by far the best after-dinner speaker I ever heard ... when he made that elaborate speech, naming the day as the birthday of all the wondrous characters of Shakespeare's creation, especially I remember, mentioning Falstaff as "the highest, merriest, wittiest creature that never lived"'.

But the enmity between Dickens and Thackeray, though uncharacteristic in the Garrick, simmered on. It was probably bound to erupt eventually, and it did so finally – in spectacular fashion. In 1858, the year after the final instalment of Dickens's *Little Dorrit* (which Thackeray had dismissed as 'damned rot') had been published, a tumultuous row broke out between Thackeray and a young journalist called Edmund Yates, who was a friend and admirer of Dickens.

The son of a distinguished actress, Yates had become a member of the Garrick as a teenager (some later suggested before the regulation age of eighteen), and was a cheerful, free and easy member, who, by his own admission, 'lived on his wits'. He wrote novels, essays, 'dramas and farces' as well as acting as a theatre critic, Christmas story writer and picture caption expert for whichever publication paid him.

Yates was one of a new breed of members that had begun to join the Garrick as Victoria's reign settled into its stride. A little less respectful than some of his predecessors, he managed to antagonise some of the older members, including Barham and Hook, not least for his column 'Lounger at the Clubs' in the *Illustrated Times*, but nevertheless had his supporters – who applauded his energy and enthusiasm for the Club. 'He was of a most sanguine cast of mind, and seemed never discouraged', wrote one, not long afterwards.

As one of a string of jobs, the then twenty-six-year-old Yates had been asked to contribute a column to a weekly called *Town Talk*, and during the second week of his engagement, on 12 June 1858, was summoned to the office late one evening to write some extra copy. Under the title 'Literary Talk' he obliged – with a portrait of Thackeray and the 'choice spirit of the Garrick Club'. 'Mr Thackeray is 46 years old, though from the whiteness of his hair he appears somewhat older. He is very tall, standing upwards of six feet two inches, and as he walks erect his height makes him conspicuous in every assembly. His face is bloodless and not particularly expressive', Yates wrote, 'but remarkable for the fracture of the bridge of his nose, the result of an accident in youth.'

'His bearing is cold and uninviting', Yates went on, 'his style of conversation either openly cynical or affectedly good-natured and benevolent; his bonhomie is forced; his wit biting; his pride easily touched; but his appearance is invariably that of a cool, suave, well-bred gentleman, who, whatever may be rankling within, suffers no surface display of his emotion'. After praising some of his writing, Yates concluded by attacking the novelist's recent lectures on English humorists, saying: 'The prices were extravagant; the lecturer's adulation of birth and position was extravagant; the success was extravagant. No one succeeds better than Mr Thackeray in cutting his coat according to his cloth: here he flattered the aristocracy; but when he crossed the Atlantic, George Washington became the idol of his worship; the "four Georges" the object of his bitterest attack ... There is a want of heart in all he writes, which is not to be balanced by the most brilliant sarcasm and the most perfect knowledge of the workings of the human heart'.

The effect was instantaneous. Thackeray was furious, and only too aware that he had never encountered Yates anywhere but at the Garrick. Where else could the young man have found the material for this distinctly unflattering portrait other than within the supposedly confidential confines of the Club? Two days after publication Thackeray replied, in a bitter letter to Yates from his house at 36 Onslow Square. 'As I understand your phrases', he wrote, 'you impute insincerity to me when I speak good-naturedly in private; assign dishonourable motives to me for sentiments which I have delivered in public, and charge me with advancing statements which I have never delivered at all'.

Thackeray could not contain himself: 'Had your remarks been written by a person unknown to me I should have noticed them no more than other calumnies; but as we have shaken hands more than once, and met hitherto on friendly terms ... I am obliged to take notice of articles which I consider not offensive and unfriendly merely, but slanderous and untrue'. And then he got to the crux of his complaint: 'We meet at a Club, where, before you were born I believe, I and other gentlemen have been in the habit of talking without any idea that our conversation would supply paragraphs for professional vendors of "Literary Talk"; and I don't remember that out of the Club I have ever exchanged six words with you'. Thackeray ended up warning

Yates off any further discussion of his 'private conversations' and his 'private affairs', and insisted that in future Yates should 'consider any question of my personal truth and sincerity as quite out of the province of your criticism'.

At this point Yates could, and probably should, have apologised without reservation, and the matter would have been at an end. But the twenty-six-year-old found Thackeray's letter 'intentionally arrogant and offensive' and decided to reply in equally frank terms. It was his club too after all. Yates decided to remind Thackeray of his 'most wanton, reckless and aggravated personality' and of some of his failings.

Yates duly drafted a letter, but decided to show it to his friend, and mentor, Dickens, before sending it. In spite of Dickens's suspicion of Thackeray, the novelist persuaded Yates not to send the brutal letter he had drafted, and instead suggested a rather less belligerent line. But Yates certainly didn't grovel. 'If your letter to me were not both "slanderous and untrue"', he wrote, I should readily have discussed its subject with you, and avowed my earnest and frank desire to set right anything I may have left wrong.'

Yates's letter was petrol on the flames. To his, and probably Dickens's, astonishment, Thackeray immediately referred their correspondence to the Club's General Committee, of which they were both members. In a letter of 19 June 1858 he insisted that 'the practice of publishing such articles' could be 'fatal to the comfort of the Club' and was 'intolerable in a society of gentlemen'. Yates had thought the matter was private but now the whole Club was drawn into the uproar. It was to engulf the Garrick for months.

The Club's Secretary, Alexander Doland, replied immediately telling Thackeray that the Committee had called a special meeting the following Saturday afternoon at 3.30 to consider his complaint. He also wrote to Yates to explain what was about to happen. Yates was furious. He wrote back insisting that it was none of the Committee's or the Garrick's business. Thackeray's grievance about the article had nothing whatever to do with the Club.

'That article makes no reference to the Club', Yates maintained, 'refers to no conversation that took place there, violates no confidence reposed there'. He admitted that the piece 'may be in exceedingly bad taste', but pointed out that the Garrick Committee 'is not a Committee of taste'. Yates had a point. There had been a string of strong remarks made by one member about another in print, but none of them had ever reached the Committee. But Thackeray was special, and held in the warmest regard by many of the senior members, some of whom were on the Committee.

One member of the Committee, however, was Charles Dickens, and when they met on Saturday 26 June 1858 Dickens was not slow to make his feelings known. Indeed he wrote to his friend, *The Times*'s correspondent William Howard Russell, then in the Crimea: 'Frightful mess, muddle, complication and botheration ensue – which witch's broth is now in full boil. You are better with a turban round your head over there, than here, with all this nonsense going on'.

But sentiment in the Club was against Dickens. The Committee decided that Thackeray's complaints were well founded and called on Yates either to 'make an ample apology' or 'to retire from the Club'. And if he failed to do either they would 'call a General Meeting ... to consider this subject'. Incensed, Yates declined to apologise to Thackeray or retire from the Garrick. A General Meeting was duly called, and it accepted by seventy votes to forty-six that the Committee had been right to judge the issue, agreed with Thackeray that the article was 'fatal to the comfort of the Club', and endorsed the Committee's view that Yates should apologise or retire. Every member of the Committee voted to support those decisions – with one exception, Charles Dickens.

Dickens's relentless energy, and his determination to give public readings of his work both in the English provinces and America, did not make him the most placid member; besides, these were hardly the happiest times for the journalist-turned-author. His marriage to Catherine was on the brink of collapse, while his affair with the young actress Ellen Ternan had scan-

dalised literary London, as had his close relationship to his sister-
in-law and housekeeper Georgina.

After the meeting Dickens was so appalled by the Club's
decision that he resigned for the second time, and left London in
disgust. But his disappearance did nothing to alleviate the situation. Yates still refused to apologise, and two weeks later the Club
formally removed his name from the list of members. But the
young freelance was not to be moved. He took legal advice about
the Club's right to remove him as a member and found a barrister prepared not only to say that they were wrong, but that he
should present himself at the Club.

There followed one of the more bizarre spectacles in the
history of the Garrick. On the steps of the old clubhouse in King
Street the Secretary prevented Yates from entering the building,
and a few days later did so again – only this time Yates had his
solicitor with him to witness the event, because he was intent on
taking the Club to court for refusing him membership. One person who did everything he could to dissuade the 'naturally intem-
perate' Yates from doing any such thing was Dickens.

Indeed in November, Dickens even tried to persuade
Thackeray that this legal argument would only harm the Garrick.
He wrote to his fellow author from his house in Tavistock Square.
'Can any conference be held between me, as representing Mr
Yates, and an appointed friend of yours, as representing you', he
asked, 'with the hope and purpose of some quiet accommodation
of this deplorable matter, which will satisfy the feelings of all concerned'. Dickens went on to admit that Yates had discussed his
original letters to Thackeray with him, and that he had argued in
the Committee that the letters were nothing to do with the Club.
He concluded optimistically: 'If this mediation that I have suggested can take place, I shall be heartily glad to do my best in it
– and God knows in no hostile spirit towards any one, least of all
you'.

That was certainly not how Thackeray saw it. Astonished
that Dickens had been Yates's advisor, he referred his letter – and
the suggested mediation – to the Committee of the Garrick. 'It is
for them to judge if any reconciliation is possible with your

friend', he wrote frostily to Dickens. The Committee did not think there was, and the matter gradually faded. In the end Yates did not feel he could afford the '£200 to £300' it would cost him to go to the Court of Chancery, and the Garrick survived.

But not without wounds – indeed Thackeray and Dickens barely spoke to each other for the next five years. If one caught sight of the other he would immediately decide to go to another room in the Club, and they would never sit beside each other at supper. Dickens was eventually readmitted as a member, but Yates remained excluded – though that did nothing to prevent him from publishing a pamphlet on the events, a copy of which remains in the Club library. To his dying day, Yates never forgave the Garrick for interfering in what he firmly believed was a private disagreement.

Not that Yates disappeared entirely into obscurity. His career in journalism prospered, and he helped C.L. Dodgson choose the pseudonym Lewis Carroll for his story about Alice's adventures. Some credit Yates with inventing the press interview, and others with establishing what some call 'Society' journalism, but the truth remains that he never really fulfilled his promise, and after the affair at the Garrick he was always somehow spoiling for a fight.

Indeed, while editor of *The World* he was sentenced to four months in prison for libelling the Earl of Lonsdale, an experience from which he never fully recovered. Ironically, it was during a first night at the Garrick Theatre that he was last sighted. By then thin and haggard, he was seen fumbling for his top hat in the stalls after the play was over. Yates was having a heart attack, and in spite of being taken to the Savoy Hotel, he died within the hour. When the news reached the Garrick Club itself that evening, 'a gloom fell upon the company', in spite of the old feud, until one member murmured: 'I wonder who'll edit the paper in his absence'. The spell was broken.

It was not until the middle of December 1863 that Dickens and Thackeray acknowledged one another again. They happened to be crossing the hall of the Athenaeum, of which both were also members, and were about to studiously ignore each other – when, quite spontaneously, they stopped and shook hands. Just two weeks later, on 30 December, Thackeray died at the age of just fifty-two.

Dickens, then fifty-one, was to remain a member of the Garrick for fifteen months after his rival's death, until another dispute over membership saw him resign for the third and final time. Once again it was the Committee that inflamed Dickens's temper. In February 1865, W.H. Wills, who had long acted as Dickens's general assistant and literary factotum, came up for membership with the vigorous support of the great novelist. Whether because of Dickens's attitude to the Committee over the Yates affair, or his disagreement with Thackeray, or because the Committee did not feel that Wills was of sufficient literary distinction is not clear, but Wills was blackballed. Dickens was outraged, and resigned at once – never to return – while Wilkie Collins (author of *The Woman in White* and one of Dickens's candidates for membership) resigned at the same moment as a gesture of support to his friend. The two men never resumed their membership, and Dickens only survived another five years before dying suddenly in 1870 at the age of fifty-eight.

THE GARRICK CLUB

Abbott, William, Esq.

Of Covent Garden Theatre, a remarkably pleasant and good-humoured man. Married a sister of Mr. Kennets, of Dover, with whom he had some property, but lost the greater part of it in a theatrical speculation as manager of the Dublin Theatre. On his afterwards going to France, I, having met him previously at Lord W. Lennox's, gave him an introductory letter to Galignani, through whom he became manager of the English Company at Paris. He afterwards returned to England and took the Victoria Theatre. Failed, and again left England.

Abbott, George Washington, Esq.

Brother to the preceding.

I   A

5

New Home

UNLIKE Thackeray, Dickens did live to see the opening of the Garrick's new home. Covent Garden's maze of tiny cobbled alleyways and streets in the area around Seven Dials was to be cleared by the Metropolitan Board of Works, who determined that a new, wider street should connect the Strand to the south with Leicester Square.

The old Probatt's Hotel at 35 King Street was always described as 'cosy' and 'intimate' but, as the size of the membership increased steadily from the original 100 founders to more than 300, it had become a little too cosy for some. Indeed the kitchens, which had hardly been satisfactory when it opened in 1831, were struggling desperately with the increased demand by the time the battle over Yates divided the Club. There had been grumbles from members about the lack of bathrooms, and the absence of a billiard table, not to mention the overcrowding and the 'intolerable heat' rising from the gas fire in the smaller of the two dining rooms.

With the redevelopment around Seven Dials proceeding apace in February 1860, the Committee decided to consider how they could improve the conditions in the clubhouse. In May a sub-committee reported that the King Street premises couldn't be enlarged and the best solution was to start from scratch on a site as nearby as possible, so that they could remain close to Drury Lane – where the Club had held its first meeting almost thirty years before.

Not that every member was all that enthusiastic about the possibility of moving from King Street, no matter how crowded. For some of the founders the possibility that this one stable element in their lives might be removed was almost too much to consider. But eventually their fears were quelled, and the Club decided to build itself a new home. It was to cost £15,000, a sum that would be raised by issuing debentures. The new building was to be designed by the superintending architect of the Metropolitan Board of Works, Frederick Marrable.

By midsummer 1862 the builders were clearing the rubble and ancient detritus from warehouses barely 200 yards from King Street and starting work on the brickwork for a building that would have a street frontage of 96 feet and be constructed in the 'Italian style'. Marrable coped with the higgledy-piggledy nature of the back of the building with great skill, and gave the new clubhouse the feeling of a small country house smack in the middle of theatreland, an atmosphere it has never lost. The entrance was not in the centre, but nearer the west end of the building to allow for a magnificent dining room, 49 feet by 26 feet. There was also 'a noble staircase of carved oak', as one contemporary newspaper report put it, as well as two bathrooms.

Even as the work progressed, however, there were still rumblings from the members. Some felt there would have to be a radical increase in new members to help pay the rent, and others didn't want to leave the familiar world of King Street – even if it was suffocating, and smelt of gas. Throughout May 1864 there was a string of angry meetings, threats of resignation, fraught scenes and general alarms, culminating in a General Meeting for all the Club's members on 21 May to consider the resignation of three Committee members, twenty-four ex-Committee members and two of the Garrick's three Trustees – in whose name the whole organization was run. The meeting was held in the new Club building, even though it was not ready for occupation.

No fewer than 158 members turned up to discuss these contentious issues under the chairmanship of the Senior Trustee, Sir Charles Russell, founder of what was to become a renowned firm of London solicitors. In the end, after a series of motions, a typically Garrick compromise was reached. All the threatened resignations were withdrawn, and the debenture holders were placated – indeed they later even wrote to say that the meeting was 'inconsistent with the social interest, welfare and security of the Club'. Not a word was mentioned about the row again.

In place of argument there was a rush to finish off the building and take up occupancy, and on 5 September 1864 King Street was closed after one of the Committee, John Arden, had supervised the removal of the picture collection and the contents of the Library. The finances were precarious for some years, and the membership had to increase to take the strain, but the Club has remained on the same site from that day to this.

It even gave its name to the street. The Metropolitan Board of Works had wanted to call it New King Street, even though the Club itself had suggested Shakespeare Street. That was not acceptable, but after a certain amount of huffing and puffing, the Board accepted the inevitable. The Garrick's new clubhouse was the dominant building in the new street, and it therefore made sense to call it Garrick Street.

There was a proposal in 1904 to move from the hurly-burly of Covent Garden to the more sedate clubland atmosphere of St James's, but in the end the members felt they had no need to be too close to the Athenaeum, or indeed the Travellers and the Reform, and voted by a considerable majority to remain exactly where they were. Twenty odd years later, in 1925, the Committee also decided to buy the freehold of the land for £23,000, as there were only seventeen years of the original eighty-year lease left to run. The Garrick's future on Garrick Street was assured.

THE GARRICK CLUB

Hobhouse, Sir John Cam, Bart, M.P.

For Westminster, afterwards Secretary of State.

Hoffman, James, Esq., F.S.A.

The confectioner.

Hook, Theodore E., Esq.

The celebrated wit, and editor of the *John Bull* paper, *New Monthly Magazine*, &c. &c.

Jerdan, William, Esq., F.S.A., M.R.S.L.

Editor of the *Literary Gazette*.

Jones, Richard, Esq.

Of Covent Garden Theatre. A very gentlemanly man. He realised a handsome competency, and, retiring from the stage, gave lessons in reading and oratory to clergymen and others.

35

~6~

Trollope and the
Pre-Raphaelites

S ETTLING into Marrable's new clubhouse didn't turn out to
be quite as difficult as many members feared. Walking up the
stone steps from the porter's lodge and through the swing
doors into the tiled hallway, the Coffee Room on the left quickly
established itself as the centre of the Club's life, while to the right
there was a Smoking Room where members could retire to read,
sleep or talk to their colleagues. At the top of the oak staircase
there was a magnificent morning room to the right, a library
directly opposite, and a card room to the left. All are still there to
this day, though some have rather different uses.

As the dust from the move began to settle and the memory of the Thackeray and Dickens furore began to fade, an air of
tranquillity descended on the Garrick. Now firmly established as
one of London's leading clubs – though without the cachet of
White's or Boodle's – its members became a little more expansive
and rather less prone to fits of self-doubt. And they all seemed, as
now, to enjoy one another's company.

No member demonstrated this more than Anthony Trollope. This shy Post Office civil servant, who gave the world the pillarbox, had only returned to England from Ireland two years previously when he was elected a member in 1861, at the age of forty-six. 'Having up to that time lived very little among men', he wrote in his posthumously published autobiography two decades later, 'having known hitherto nothing of clubs, having even as a boy been banished from social gatherings, I enjoyed infinitely the gaiety of the Garrick'.

Trollope was to become as much a pillar of the Club as Thackeray had been before him. Indeed, just two years after his election, he was invited to take Thackeray's place on the Committee after the great man's death, and he went on to become one of the three Club Trustees. The Garrick became a passion. 'It was a festival to me to dine there ... and a great delight to play a rubber in the little room upstairs of an afternoon. When I began to play at the Garrick, I did so simply because I liked the society of the men who played. I think I became popular among those with whom I associated'. The self-deprecating Trollope had found his home. As he put it himself: 'I have long been aware of a certain weakness in my character, which I may call a craving for love. I have ever wished to be liked by those around me – a wish that during the first half of my life was never gratified ... The Garrick Club was the first assemblage of men at which I felt myself to be popular'.

Many other Garrick members over the years have felt exactly the same way. To many the Club satisfies a craving of one kind or another, be it love, affection, warmth, friendship or a sense of belonging. But Trollope's undoubted popularity spurred him on to complete his Barsetshire series of novels, and then create the now acclaimed political Palliser series. Unrelentingly hard-working, he produced no fewer than forty-seven novels, several travel books, biographies (including one of Thackeray) and collections of short stories before his death in 1882 at the age of sixty-seven.

When proposing the first historian of the Club, Percy Fitzgerald, whose history was published in 1904, Trollope commented that his proposer had to 'undergo the mortifying process of being gradually let down' as his popularity among the reading public – rather than among Club members – began to wane. But his delight in the Garrick never deserted him. Burly and boisterous, one fellow member at the time described his 'frank, but aggressive cordiality'. Fitzgerald shrewdly commented later: 'This manner of his always struck me as being somewhat affected, assumed to hide either shyness or a certain feeling of not being at ease'. Even today members might notice just such a tendency in themselves.

Not that Trollope was the only luminary in the Club. One of his most distinguished contemporaries, also a friend of Thackeray, was Lord Leighton. 'Handsome and distinguished in presence', according to another of the Club's historians, Guy Boas, 'his old-world courtesy and modesty were an adornment to the Club'. As an infant the Scarborough-born Frederic Leighton had 'toured Europe in a perambulator', and at twenty-five, in 1855, he settled in Rome where his famously cultivated manners brought him many friends, including the French novelist George Sand and the poet Robert Browning. He returned to London in 1860, and became a member of the Garrick shortly afterwards. In 1869 he was made a member of the Royal Academy, becoming its President nine years later. In 1886 he was made a baronet, and – on the day before he died – became the first English painter to be made a member of the House of Lords when he was created Lord Leighton of Stretton.

Leighton was not the only artist of distinction in the Garrick at the time, however. On his election to the Club Thackeray had written to another artist member, John Everett Millais, who was just a year older than Leighton: 'Here's a versatile young dog, who will run you close for the presidentship one of these days'. Millais, who formed the Pre-Raphaelite Brotherhood together with Dante Gabriel Rossetti and William Holman Hunt in 1848 when he was only nineteen, was a precocious talent. But he had to wait until 1885 to be made a baronet and 1896 before he did finally follow Leighton as President of the Royal Academy, only to die in office in August, just two months after Leighton.

Both keen billiards players, a portrait of the two men — among many other members — hangs in the Club's Billiard Room to this day; but while the Garrick does not own any works by Leighton it does possess two striking ones by Millais, portraits of actors Sir John Hare and, of course, Sir Henry Irving, a painting that now hangs in the room that bears Irving's name. Millais also illustrated Trollope's later works, and, like Trollope, became one of the three Trustees. 'Millais loved the Club', recorded Squire Bancroft at the time, 'and cared but little for any other'. But he was not the only Pre-Raphaelite to become a member. Rossetti was elected in 1865 and Millais's lifelong friend Hunt not long afterwards. The Brotherhood met regularly in the Club's new Garrick Street building. Indeed Hunt was to remain a member of the Garrick until his death in 1910 at the age of eighty-three.

In 1864 Millais and Trollope supported the candidature of another novelist and stalwart of the Garrick, George Meredith, whose most famous novel, *The Egotist*, was to be published in 1879. The son of a flamboyant and extravagant tailor from Portsmouth, his literary career began after he had worked for a firm of solicitors, when he published his first book of poems, a volume that he later disowned but was nevertheless praised for by Tennyson. A signed copy of his excellent political novel *Beauchamp's Career*, published in 1876, still remains in the Club's library. And by the time of his death, in 1909, Meredith had been awarded the Order of Merit as well as being President of the Society of Authors, a man of letters sought out by younger poets and novelists, including Henry James and Thomas Hardy.

Things were not always quite as amicable as they seemed, however. One of the most notable creative partnerships of the nineteenth century, Gilbert and Sullivan was divided rather than united by the Garrick. Arthur Sullivan joined at the age of twenty-four in 1869, and remained a member until his death in 1900, at the age of fifty-eight. 'The Garrick', one member wrote, 'was Sullivan's Club-home. To the end of his days he clung to the Garrick, which held his friends, and the atmosphere of which was his own'. It may have included his friends, but his collaborator on the Savoy operas, William S. Gilbert was certainly not among them.

David Garrick by Johan Zoffany (Cat. G0249)

Charles Mathews playing four of his characters and as himself by George Henry Harlow
(Cat. G0471)

Edmund Kean, George Clint, John Pritt Harley, Joseph Shepherd Munden and others in *A New Way to Pay Old Debts*, by George Clint (Cat. G0355)

Sir Charles Taylor and Garrick Club members in the Billiard Room by Henry O'Neil (Cat. G0793)

William Makepeace Thackeray by Daniel Maclise

Charles Dickens after Daniel Maclise (Cat. G0155)

Anthony Trollope by Henry O'Neil (Cat. G0821)

Sir William Gilbert by Sir John Herbert
von Herkomer (Cat. G0263)

Sir John Everett Millais by 'Spy' (Cat. G0605)

Dame Ellen Terry, Sir Herbert Beerbohm Tree and Dame Madge Kendal in *The Merry Wives of Windsor*, by John Collier (Cat. G0820)

Sir Charles Wyndham as David Garrick by John Pettie (Cat. G0860)

Sir Henry Irving by Sir John Everett Millais (Cat. G0323)

Significantly, Gilbert was not elected a member until 1906, six years after Sullivan's death. But the fault was not entirely Sullivan's. Certainly there were some members of the Committee who felt that – after the partnership finally broke up in the wake of *The Grand Duke* in 1896 – Sullivan might have been embarrassed to run into his lyricist in the Club. But there was a further reason. Another member, the then editor of the weekly humorous magazine *Punch*, Frank Burnand, had been replaced by Gilbert as Sullivan's librettist before the success of *Trial By Jury* and the other operettas, and he had never forgiven him. Burnand did everything in his power to make sure that Gilbert did not become a member during Sullivan's lifetime, although when he was eventually put up as a candidate his signature was among those of Gilbert's supporters.

Almost every editor of *Punch* became a member of the Garrick. Mark Lemon, the first editor and one of the Club's founders, was elected in 1854, Tom Taylor and Shirley Brooks, later editors, in 1850, Sir Frank Burnand, was in post for twenty-six years, in 1865, and Sir Owen Seaman, who also did the job for twenty-six years, in 1906. *Punch*'s cartoonists too held sway in the Club. John Leech, a contemporary of Thackeray's at Charterhouse, arrived in 1849, and worked ceaselessly for *Punch*, as well as illustrating the Christmas books of Dickens. The Club possesses twenty-five of his drawings, as well as a striking self-portrait in pencil.

But the Garrick tradition of raffishness – even loucheness – was much in evidence in the second half of the nineteenth century. In April 1857, for example, a certain Mr Percy Boyd of Ryde in the Isle of Wight was sternly rebuked by the Secretary for not paying his subscriptions, and reminded that this was not the first time it had happened. But that was by no means Mr Boyd's only transgression. It seems that he was also in the habit of borrowing money from the staff: 'a course of conduct which the Committee hold to be amongst the most objectionable of which a member can be guilty'.

Boyd was incensed and replied at great length, insisting that it was 'common practice' to use the servants as 'temporary bankers', adding: 'I am anxious for an opportunity for a personal explanation in the presence of whoever has thus misrepresented me'. As the last Club historian, Richard Hough, remarked later: 'That was a very foolish thing to write', for it exasperated the Committee who launched a thorough investigation. It turned out that Mr Boyd had been doing it for a very long time indeed. 'You are at this moment', the Secretary wrote, 'in debt to every single male servant in the Establishment, from the Steward to the Messenger …' Mr Boyd was promptly expelled.

Mr Charles Hambro's crime was no less serious. Elected in May 1860, he brought a guest to the Club a few days later, but left without paying his bill, his entrance fee, or his subscription. The Committee called that sort of behaviour 'unjustifiable' and 'unprecedented'; but Hambro rapidly made amends, paid, and survived as a member.

Another disreputable character, John Litton, a Dublin barrister ran him close, however. He was in the habit of paying for dinner with cheques that bounced. Indeed, in January 1873, in spite of being warned and told specifically that he had to pay in cash, Litton settled his account with a cheque drawn on Messrs Coutts & Co of nearby 440 The Strand. The cheque was returned to the Club with a note explaining that the account had been closed for some time. A distinctly unimpressed Committee responded by 'erasing' Mr Litton from the list of members.

But the spectre of envy that had stalked the Club, and seen Burnand keep out W.S. Gilbert, then reappeared in a scandal that was to shake the Garrick, and its connections with actors, to its very foundations. The new young star of the London stage, thirty-three-year-old Henry Irving, was put up for membership in the wake of his sensational success in the melodrama *The Bells*. Irving had been toiling in the provinces for years, but had finally made his breakthrough in the West End, with extensive queues as a result. Irving's name came before the Committee in the early autumn of 1873, and everyone confidently expected him to be elected with acclaim.

Astonishingly, Irving was blackballed. One member of the Committee, all of whom had to vote to accept a new member in those days, voted against him in the secret ballot. No one knew which member had objected at the time – but the effect was dramatic. Irving was stunned, and so was the acting profession. The cream of London's theatre world, many of whom were fully expecting to be put up and become members of the Garrick as their careers extended, suddenly took fright and would not risk the possibility that they too might find themselves blackballed. Indeed so great was the scandal it was to be fully another sixteen years before another major name on the London stage would allow himself to be proposed for membership of the Club.

Thanks to the researches of a current member, Richard Bebb, we now know who blackballed Irving. It was another actor – the bearded, Scottish-born James Anderson, who can be seen in his shirtsleeves playing pool in the famous Billiard Room painting of the match of 1869. He is right in the middle of the painting. Anderson was the doyen of the actor members of the Garrick at the time, and felt that Irving was an upstart who could turn out to be little more than a flash in the pan, and who certainly hadn't done enough in London to justify membership of the Garrick. There must also be the suspicion that Anderson did not want to be upstaged in his own Club.

Irving, however, was made of sterner stuff. With the support of Trollope, who was appalled at the blackball, as well as fellow actors Squire Bancroft and Sir John Hare, not to mention Sullivan, he allowed his name to be put forward a second time, six months after the disastrous blackball. And on 21 March 1874 Irving was finally elected, and his 'page' in the candidates' book – which is covered with more than fifty signatures – is on display in the hall of the Club to this day. Those who look at the display a little more closely will see that it is a case – and if the case is opened Irving's previous candidate's page will be found behind it: the one that certifies his blackball.

If one person was to dominate the Garrick in the last quarter of the nineteenth century it was without question Sir Henry Irving. Indeed so strong was his influence, and so profound his love of the Club, that it resonates through the Coffee Room even now. If the spirit of Kemble imbued the Club's first fifty years, and if the novelists Thackeray, Dickens and Trollope dominated until 1874, it was Irving who ushered in the era of the actors, and established the Garrick's reputation as the Club that all leading actors wished to belong to. He himself, though, was for some time one of the only actors in the Club at the pinnacle of the profession until the stigma of his first blackball had finally been erased from the memory of his fellow actors in London.

∽7∾

Irving

J OHN HENRY Brodribb was born on 6 February 1838 in the Somerset village of Keinton Mandeville. His father Samuel was a salesman who collected orders for the tailoring department of a local store and his mother Mary came from a farming family in Cornwall. When he was four his father got a job in Bristol, but rather than risk his son's health in the damp and dirt of the city, decided to send his son to his wife's sister Sarah who lived near St Ives. He stayed there for six years before rejoining his parents, who by now had moved to London.

After leaving school he got a job as a clerk in a merchant's office, but his real interest was the theatre, and at the age of eighteen a £100 legacy from an uncle enabled him to buy the theatrical necessities of the time: wigs, swords, costumes, and the leading part in an amateur production of *Romeo and Juliet* at the Royal Soho Theatre. For his first appearance he chose the stage name Irving, a choice determined by his admiration for the romances of Washington Irving and the sermons of the Scottish preacher Edward Irving.

Henry Irving's Romeo was sufficiently well received to encourage him to give up clerking and join a theatrical company in Sunderland as a 'walking gentleman'. It was here that he served his apprenticeship as an actor, playing more than 500 parts in 330 plays, including most, but not quite all, of Shakespeare's canon. He toured the English provinces for a decade before coming to London in a play called *Hunted Down* in 1866. It was a mild success, but not enough to persuade him to stay. Irving went back to touring.

In Dublin the following year he was introduced to Florence O'Callaghan, the daughter of an Irish surgeon-general, and the couple were married in July 1869. Their first son Henry was born the next year, and their second, Laurence, in 1871, but by that time the couple had separated after a quarrel over the first night of what was to become Irving's first major success, *The Bells*. Legend has it that Florence was upset by a remark on their way home in a Hackney carriage — that 'in future they would be able to afford their own carriage'. She reproached him for his extravagance. Irving was horrified, stopped the Hackney, got out, and never saw her again.

In fact *The Bells* only came about because the American impresario H.L. Bateman had been looking for a leading man to play opposite his daughter Isabel and had chosen Irving. The pair's first efforts hadn't met with tremendous success, partly because Isabel was no great actress. But then Irving discovered *The Bells*, and persuaded the American to finance it, with him as Mathias, an unconvicted murderer haunted by his conscience. It perfectly suited Irving's gift for the melodramatic and the macabre and became, quite literally, a sensation at the Lyceum Theatre, which was not far away down the Strand from the Garrick Club.

Over the next four years Irving became the star of Bateman's company, and — after the setback of the blackball — was also elected to the Garrick Club. His portrayal of Hamlet in the autumn after his election sealed his place at the pinnacle of British acting. Not every critic liked his reading of the prince as a man whose failure to act came from an excess of tenderness rather than weakness, but the theatregoing public adored it.

When Bateman died in 1875, Irving continued to play under the management of his widow for a further two years, until he himself took over the lease of the Lyceum and the management of his own company. It was then that he invited the exquisite Ellen Terry to join him as his leading lady, forming one of the most famous partnerships in the history of the English stage – he the brooding introvert, she the spontaneous, impulsive creature who won the audience's heart. As Hamlet and Ophelia, Shylock and Portia they drew enormous audiences.

The mixture of an incandescent personality, coupled with an undeniable internal sadness, might explain why he came to mean so much to the Garrick, and the Club so much to him. As Guy Boas put it: 'domination, electric, almost mesmeric, was the profession, the life force, of that stupendous and uncanny personality'. The man who had frozen the blood of audiences as Richard III and Mephistopheles and wrung their hearts as Charles I and Thomas Becket rapidly became the very centre of the Garrick's life.

At about 11.45 each evening, the performance at the Lyceum behind him, Irving would appear in the Club's Coffee Room, often alone, but sometimes with one or two guests, ready for a late night. Another actor member, G.P. Bancroft, recalled afterwards: 'He would stroll quite unselfconsciously to the desk to order his haddock or kidneys, but I can feel it now as I did then. Literally a hush fell on the room, and every eye at the table, be it young or old, would follow that man from the door to the desk. No other figure of the theatre of that epoch or perhaps of any other would command that'. The playwright Sir Arthur Pinero, another member whose own eminence almost came to rival Irving's, agreed. 'Such were Irving's inherent gifts', he wrote, 'his determination and his infinite patience, that there was no walk in life in which he could not have succeeded. He was the most dignified figure in any assembly, no matter how eminent.'

Not that Irving was without flaw. He could be withering when he chose to, and he did not take kindly to members leaving his company at the centre table. When someone sitting nearby got up to go while he was still in full flood he would remark, in that unmistakable dark brown voice: 'I regret, Sir, that you are fatigued by our company'. It was a brave member who would risk the rebuke.

Fellow actors were also liable to feel the back of Irving's tongue. One night he was dining at the Club with Richard Mansfield, who was playing Richard III at the Old Globe Theatre. Mansfield staggered into the Club, and threw himself – exhausted – into the chair beside Irving. 'What on earth's the matter?', one or two members enquired. 'I've been playing Richard', replied Mansfield breathing heavily, 'Terrible strain you know, terrible strain'. There was a pause. Irving looked across the centre table and said quietly: 'My boy, if unwholesome, why do it?'

But Irving could also be the most gracious host, in the least likely circumstances, especially when the conversation had nothing to do with the theatre. One member later recorded the occasion when the journalist and explorer Henry Morton Stanley, immortal discoverer of Dr Livingstone, was invited to the Club as Irving's guest. When the cigars arrived Irving reclined in his chair at the head of the Garrick's long centre table and announced: 'My dear fellow, you must tell us about your adventures – your wanderings – in – um – Africa'.

Stanley launched into a vastly overlong monologue. As one member recalled: 'His sentences were so deliberate that those who tried to hang on his lips soon fell back in their chairs: the Ancient Mariner with his story was not in it with Stanley'. Members slowly began to slip away, and as they did so Irving slid further and further down in his chair until his head was touching the chair back, all the time keeping his eyes closed. He would occasionally nod, or open his eyes, only to resume his position. Stanley's description of his exploits on the Dark Continent lasted until the early hours of the morning, by which time only Irving and one other member remained. 'Most interesting, most interesting', Irving said as he ushered his guest out of the Club.

Throughout the 1880s Irving's Lyceum company was at the height of its financial success, embarking on a triumphant American tour in 1883, though the young critic George Bernard Shaw wondered why Ellen Terry would waste her talents on what he called 'ponderous trifles' – the forgettable plays that Irving often chose for them. Shaw had written a play, *The Man of Destiny*, which he hoped the pair would appear in. Irving read it, gave

Shaw a retainer, and forgot all about it. Shaw accused him of trying to suppress the play, and the two became antagonists.

When Queen Victoria knighted Irving in July 1895, he
became the first English actor ever to be accorded the honour,
and also the target of Shaw's anger. At the same time the critic
and aspiring playwright was trying to persuade Irving – through
Ellen Terry – to consider the work of the Norwegian playwright
Henrik Ibsen. Terry managed to cajole Irving into reading two
acts of *John Gabriel Borkman*, only for the actor-manager to retort:
'Threadworms and leeches are an interesting study, but they have
no interest to me'. Irving's success had been based on the 'actor's
theatre' where the dramatist was the servant of the performer, and
he saw no reason to change his approach. The 'author's theatre'
was yet to come.

Tragically, Irving's knighthood also marked the start of his
decline. Less than two years after it was awarded he suffered the
first of a series of crippling blows when a production of a play
about Peter the Great was a financial disaster. Shortly afterwards
all the stored scenery for many of his classic Lyceum productions
was destroyed by fire (the insurance being insufficient to cover the
loss), and finally, in 1898, Irving suffered – at the age of sixty –
his first serious illness. It meant that he couldn't tour with his
company, and the box office suffered in consequence. The final
years of his life were a struggle to keep his company afloat – and
he failed. In 1902 it went into liquidation and his thirty-one-year
reign at the Lyceum came to an end. Irving, of course, continued
to act, and to go to the Garrick, just as he had always done, but
the flame that had once burned so brightly was beginning to dim.

Irving's devotion to the Club, and the Club's to him, is perfectly demonstrated in two paintings. In 1889 Irving presented the
Garrick with George Clint's magnificent portrait of Edmund
Kean playing Sir Giles Overreach in Philip Massinger's *A New
Way to Pay Old Debts* – the picture had been the centrepiece of the
Royal Academy's exhibition in 1820, but had then disappeared
into obscurity. Offered the painting by a dealer more than half a
century after its exhibition, Irving had purchased it and hung it
in the Beefsteak Room at the Lyceum. But he had decided the

Garrick was the better place for it, announcing: 'Here it is hidden away, there it will be seen by many'.

Clint's masterpiece certainly deserved to be seen, revealing as it does one of the most remarkable moments in English theatre and the climax of Kean's career: the opening night of Massinger's play on 12 January 1816. Overreach has just discovered that his plans for his daughter to marry Lord Lovell have been thwarted and that she has secretly married Allworth. In a frenzy, Overreach rushes towards his daughter intent on killing her, a moment that one of Kean's biographers describes as 'the most powerful exhibition of human passion that has ever been witnessed on the English stage'.

It certainly had an extraordinary impact on the cast and audience. Mrs Orger, who was playing Overreach's daughter Margaret, was so overcome with emotion that she collapsed on the stage of Drury Lane in genuine hysterics, another actor was carried off the stage in a trance, several lady members of the audience started screaming and had to be led from the theatre, and Lord Byron, who was in the audience, was thrown into convulsions. The painting has lost none of its power, as anyone who pauses to look at it on the staircase will attest.

The affection felt for Irving by so many members of the Garrick is only too clearly demonstrated in the portrait by Millais that now hangs above the fireplace in the room that bears Irving's name. Painted in 1883, the artist presented it to the Club the following year, and it conveys all of Irving's qualities – the 'egotism of the great type' – that his perennial leading lady always ascribed to him. The Club possesses more than twenty portraits of one of its most distinguished members, but none to match this one.

Nowhere is Irving's significance to the Club's members clearer than in his death. On the evening of 13 October 1905, Irving, by now almost penniless because of the financial travails of the previous years of his life, was playing the leading role in Alfred, Lord Tennyson's *Becket* at the Theatre Royal, Bradford. He took his curtain call, but then collapsed in the wings – and was carried from the theatre into a cab to be taken to the Midland Hotel, where he was staying. Helped through the revolving doors he had barely taken a step when he collapsed again. Put into a chair by a helpful night porter, Irving died.

When the news reached the Garrick later that evening, the entire membership present stood in silence and left the Coffee Room as a mark of respect. Irving was buried in Poets' Corner at Westminster Abbey, and his personal effects were auctioned to help provide for his widow Florence, even though he had not seen her for more than thirty years. His obituaries called him 'The Knight from Nowhere' who left behind only the memories of his performances.

But Irving left something else. Fellow actor member Sir Seymour Hicks, whose portrait in top hat and white tie hangs in the Cocktail Bar and who had become a member in 1899, was a great admirer of Irving's, as well as a collector of theatrical memorabilia. He was on tour in the Bradford area shortly after Irving's death, and went in search of the night porter who had seen the great man draw his last breath. Hicks found him, and he also found that the porter had kept the chair in which Irving died. He had even pencilled his initials in the seat. 'I knew Sir Henry Irving was a great man', the porter reportedly told Hicks, 'and some day someone might want the chair'.

Hicks was delighted, purchased the chair, and transported it back to the Garrick. It stands guard on the second landing of the Club's main staircase to this day. No other single member in its history has dominated the Garrick quite as completely as Irving. One earlier historian of the Club suggests he may have presided over a 'dark age' when the old place lost something of its sparkle. I could not disagree more. Irving brought the Garrick actors again, after the long gap in the wake of his blackball, and he brought the Club into the limelight. How could he not? If anyone created the glamour that has come to surround it in the century that followed his death it was Irving.

THE GARRICK CLUB

Adolphus, John, Esq., F.S.A., Barrister

I first became acquainted with Mr. Adolphus at the Literary Fund Club, where he afterwards dined as my visitor and was elected a member on my nomination, but owing to ill-health he withdrew the following year; the same cause prevented his coming much to the Garrick, in the formation of which, however, he took a part, and originated the library, by proposing that every member should be requested to give his duplicate dramatic books. He was a man full of anecdote, but occasionally very rude, which made him, though a very eloquent, also a very unpopular member at the Bar, and unquestionably prevented his rising to the highest rank in his profession. He was the author of a continuation of Hume and Smollet, a book of indifferent pretensions. In early life Mr. Adolphus was a leading member of the Eccentrics, a debating society which met at the Sutherland Arms in May's Buildings. In 1837 I again became better acquainted with him in consequence of meeting him at Bentley's, for whom he was engaged to write the life of John Bannister.

2

$$\underset{\sim}{8}\underset{\smile}{}$$

The Lawyers Arrive

S
IR HENRY Irving was certainly not the only distinguished
member to grace the Club during the last quarter of the nineteenth century. Lord Rosebery, who had been Gladstone's
Foreign Secretary and become Liberal Premier in March 1894,
remaining in Downing Street until June 1895, was elected a member in March 1869. By all accounts he took refuge in the Club in
the wake of his resignation and the splintering of the Liberal
Party, before finally relinquishing its leadership in October 1896.

But the 5th Earl of Rosebery wasn't the first Prime Minister
to be a member of the Garrick. Lord John Russell, British
Premier from 1846 until 1852 and again from 1865 to 1866 had
been a member too, as had his namesake Lord Russell of
Killowen, the Lord Chief Justice of England from June 1894 until
his death in August 1900. Also a Liberal, Charles Russell had
been an MP from 1880 until 1894, serving as Gladstone's
Attorney General, after an immensely successful career at the Bar.
Russell had defended the Irish nationalist Charles Parnell, and
was later regarded as a strong, but moderate, member of the
Bench. After becoming a member of the Garrick in 1893 – where

he was always known as Frank — he went on to become one of its staunchest supporters and a Club Trustee.

Russell was one of a band of barristers who began to assert their membership of the Garrick as the century drew to a close. Lawyers of one form or another had been joining the Club since its earliest days, but as the Garrick grew stronger, so the influence of the legal profession upon it steadily increased. The writers and journalists, actors and painters, gradually found themselves outnumbered, even outgunned, by the more respectable — at least in their own eyes — lawyers.

None of the lawyer members at the time could quite match the stature of the formidable F.E. Smith, later Lord Birkenhead, but Sir Edward Marshall Hall, Lord Carson, Lord Hewart and Lord Buckmaster certainly came close. The controversial Marshall Hall, for example, who became a member of the Club in 1891, had something of a reputation for annoying the judges he appeared in front of, 'a reputation that was not altogether undeserved', commented the novelist Dornford Yates. 'But he was a very fine advocate ... He was tall and broad and a very handsome man; and he had the most splendid presence of anyone at the Bar.'

Other professions represented among the Garrick's membership had their own stars too. Thackeray and Dickens, for example, were succeeded by George Meredith, W.W. Jacobs, Arnold Bennett and Sir Hugh Walpole, while among the musicians Arthur Sullivan's mantle passed to Edward Elgar. And then came the dramatists, among them, of course, J.M. Barrie, author of *Peter Pan*, and Sir Arthur Pinero, whose generosity to the Club on his death in 1934 — he left it one third of his estate — helped the Club to survive some remarkably lean times in the future.

First elected a member in 1884, at the age of twenty-nine, Pinero had become one of the pillars of the Garrick by the turn of the nineteenth century. Leaving school at the age of ten to join his father's solicitor's practice, he had been stage-struck from an early age and decided to become an actor. Indeed he was recommended to Henry Irving by Wilkie Collins, allegedly by mistake, and joined Irving's Lyceum company in 1876. Even at the age of twenty-one Pinero certainly was not in awe of the great man. Legend has it that when Pinero sat down on some jagged scenery, Irving told him: 'Get up my boy, you will cut yourself'. Pinero promptly replied: 'Mr Irving, we are accustomed to having our parts cut in this theatre'.

Significantly it was Irving who encouraged Pinero to become a playwright. His first one-act play, *Two Hundred a Year*, was performed in 1877, and heralded what was to become a remarkably prolific career. It was his farce *The Magistrate*, first performed in 1885, that made him both famous and wealthy. Two later farces, *The Schoolmistress* of 1886 and *Sweet Lavender* of 1888, did almost as well. But it was to be Pinero's more serious plays that were to seal his reputation, almost all of them based around the theme of the double standards that applied to men and woman in late Victorian England. Indeed, it was his apparent understanding of women that brought him very considerable acclaim.

In 1893 Pinero's masterpiece *The Second Mrs Tanqueray* became a worldwide success, followed just two years later by *The Notorious Mrs Ebbsmith*, and in 1898 by *Trelawny of the Wells*, a sentimental comedy nostalgically recalling his own passion for the theatre as a boy. By the time he was knighted in 1909, however, Pinero's reputation had begun to wane with the passing of the Victorian era, and though he continued to write relentlessly for the next quarter of a century his reputation dwindled, and his sense of disillusion grew. The Garrick, as it has done for so many of its members throughout its history, provided him with the solace that he never found in the theatre again, and made him a Trustee in 1926. In the Club at least Pinero was still the man he had been at the end of the nineteenth century, and he repaid the debt handsomely with his bequest of some £20,000 in 1934, as well as a continuing share in his royalties.

With his long nose, thick eyebrows and famously bald pate, Pinero was to become as dominant in the Garrick – in his own less showy way – as Irving had been, and certainly more so than the rather more retiring Barrie, who nevertheless left the manuscript of his play, *The Will*, to the Club's library, where it remains one of its treasures – alongside the typescript of another dramatist member of the time, Harley Granville Barker's *The Voysey Inheritance.*

Born the son of a London elocution teacher in 1877 Granville Barker became an actor at the age of fourteen and quickly gained recognition. But he was more than an actor. Between 1904 and 1907 he directed, with outstanding success, seasons of plays at the new Royal Court Theatre in Sloane Square, producing Shakespeare, modern classics, including Galsworthy, and — in 1905 — his own masterpiece *The Voysey Inheritance.* Three years later he became a member of the Garrick.

Ironically Granville Barker was one of the men who ushered George Bernard Shaw into prominence, and helped the curtain descend on the reputation of his fellow Garrick member Pinero. In the years before the outbreak of the First World War he also helped to revolutionise the staging of Shakespeare — pioneering the use of an apron stage, simple settings, authentic text and swift continuity of action. He was to remain an enthusiastic member of the Garrick until his death in 1946, at the age of sixty-nine, serving the last years of his life in military intelligence.

In the wake of Irving's blackball, senior actors tended to shy away from the Garrick for almost a decade, but as Irving's star ascended higher and higher in the Club so he was succeeded there by the cream of the London stage, led by Sir Herbert Beerbohm Tree, who became a member in 1884 at the age of thirty-one. Like Irving, Tree possessed a personality so expansive that it dominated everything he touched. As Guy Boas neatly put it: 'To have seen Tree as Mark Anthony, or Irving as Richard III, was to have seen something both less than and additional to Shakespeare ... what they lacked in personal effacement they compensated for in personal force'.

Together the two men raised the status of English theatre, and drama, to new heights. Tree's Fagin and Mephistopheles, as well as his first London Hamlet in 1892, were all astonishing successes. But it was his performance as Svengali in a stage adaptation by Paul Potter of fellow Garrick member George Du Maurier's novel about his experiences as a young painter in Paris — *Trilby* — which opened on 30 October 1895 at the Theatre Royal, Haymarket that made Tree his fortune. Indeed it provided him with the funds to build his own theatre across the road, Her Majesty's. A leather-bound souvenir programme, presented at a royal performance before Queen Victoria, remains in the Club's library.

As a tribute to the Coronation celebrations for King Edward VII in 1902 Tree presented Shakespeare's *The Merry Wives of Windsor*, with Dame Ellen Terry as Mrs Page and Dame Madge Kendall as Mrs Ford. It was a typically flamboyant, lavish Tree production, with incidental music composed by his fellow member Sir Arthur Sullivan, who had died eighteen months earlier. The Honourable John Collier's stunning portrait of Tree and his two leading ladies – who had never appeared together on the same stage before – hangs in the Club's Milne Room – proof, if any were needed, of just how highly the actor was esteemed by his fellow members.

For his part Tree, like Irving, loved the Garrick. As his widow wrote shortly after his death in 1917: 'How Herbert loved it! And how proud he was when he became a member. And how many thousand times have I taken him, or called for him there'. Lady Tree also insisted: 'All his life he was the light of childish eyes' – and his fellow members always remembered him for his childlike attitude, perennially cheerful, enthusiastic, restless, at once delighted and delightful – and given to sulking. When Mrs Patrick Campbell hit him in the eye with one of Professor Higgins's slippers during the rehearsals for the original production of Shaw's *Pygmalion*, he stormed off – only to return with a sheepish grin on his face, a grin that he would also use when he and Shaw had their daily falling-out during the rehearsals.

One of Tree's friends and fellow members, Louis Parker, described him as 'the most loveable man I have ever known', and added: 'He believed in everybody until they deceived him – and then he pensioned them'. Tree was certainly not above intervening if he thought that a member was behaving badly. Sir Alfred Sutro once recalled a famous evening when Tree and Gerald Du Maurier were dining together in the Garrick, and their conversation turned to an article that reflected on the morals of actresses. In particular it suggested that by the very nature of their profession actresses' morals must be less high than those of other women. The matter was being hotly debated – and the suggestion roundly condemned – when a usually silent, but constantly bibulous member suddenly blurted out that the piece was absolutely correct and that most actresses were whores.

The Garrick's centre table fell silent. The member was clearly drunk, and so allowances had to be made, but this was too much to bear. Tree and Du Maurier retired briefly under the stairs to decide what to do. They returned and stood opposite the now rather tired, but unrepentant, member – and a hush fell. 'Look here', said Tree, tapping him on the shoulder, 'of course we know that you have had, well' – and he paused theatrically to look across at the empty bottle of champagne – 'and that you wouldn't have said it if you hadn't; but how would you like it if we declared that your sister was …'. Tree declined to repeat the word, but let the sentence hang in the air. There was a lengthy pause – until the member looked across at Tree and said quietly: 'She is'.

Two years after Tree became a member, another leading actor joined. Sir George Alexander was a far less flamboyant member than Tree; indeed he was a shy man, whom some thought of as a rather cold fish. Only twenty-eight when he joined, he was to become one of the most dashing leading men of his day, not least playing Rudolph Rassendyll in the stage version of Anthony Hope's novel *The Prisoner of Zenda*, a performance that is commemorated in Robert Brough's magnificent portrait of Alexander that hangs in the very centre of the wall behind the Cocktail Bar – dominating the room.

In life Alexander was rather less dominant a figure, but revered nonetheless. He had started his career playing minor parts under Irving's management, even touring with him in the United States, then going on to play leading roles at the Lyceum. But it was at the St James's Theatre, where he launched Oscar Wilde's *Lady Windermere's Fan* and *The Importance of Being Earnest*, that his reputation was confirmed. Two years earlier he had starred in Pinero's *The Second Mrs Tanqueray*, confirming his fellow member's reputation as a playwright, and simultaneously launching the career of Mrs Patrick Campbell.

Tall, refined, and always immaculately turned out, Alexander could appear a touch supercilious to some of his fellow members. But the Garrick is no respecter of persons, no matter how distinguished they may be. One member encountered Alexander one afternoon in a state of the greatest agitation. It turned out that someone sitting in the front row of the dress circle had emptied the stalls at the St James's the previous evening by being violently sick. 'It took place', Alexander said fiercely, 'when I was on in my big scene. What on earth can I do to prevent such an appalling thing happening again?' There was a Garrick pause. 'You must leave the stage', his fellow member told him cheerfully.

Not that Alexander was totally without a sense of humour, and the ability to appeal to the lady members of the audience. Indeed his charm certainly worked on one of the leading actresses of his time, the redoubtable, and decidedly beautiful Dame Lillian Braithwaite, whose portrait hangs not far from his in the Cocktail Bar. Rumour always had it that they were lovers, and certainly closer than Dame Lillian's husband, the actor Gerald Lawrence cared for. It is touching to see their portraits gazing across the Garrick's bar at each other even now.

One of the few actors of stature to risk becoming a member of the Garrick shortly after Irving's blackball was Sir John Hare, who joined in 1868 at the age of just twenty-four. He came to love the Club, remaining a member for more than half a century, until his death in 1921, and serving as one of its Trustees in the last years of his life. A quiet man, who was particularly fond of playing whist in the Card Room, he made a theatrical career out of playing old men. In 1881 he played Baron Croodle in *The Money Spinner*, the first of Pinero's plays to be put on in London and later produced Pinero's *The Notorious Mrs Ebbsmith*. One of his greatest triumphs was playing the impecunious Lord Kildare in *A Quiet Rubber* at the age of thirty-two in make-up that was designed to make him look at least twice his age. Hugh Goldwin Riviere's portrait of Hare in the part used to grace the Club's Card Room, in recognition of Hare's enthusiasm for the game, but in recent years it has moved to the Cocktail Bar.

One further portrait in the Bar shows another of the Club's luminaries at the end of the nineteenth century, Sir Charles Wyndham, playing Garrick himself in the comedy *David Garrick*. John Pettie's full-length oil shows Wyndham dressed in silvery green breeches and a red coat, with a white ruffle at his throat. It became the part most closely associated with the actor throughout his life, after he had seen a performance in 1864 as a young man, and sensed that it could be a perfect vehicle for his comic talent. After engaging the help of James Albery and Alfred Calmour to polish up the dialogue in Thomas William Robertson's original play, he opened at the Criterion in Piccadilly Circus in 1886, when he was almost fifty. He was to play the part repeatedly through-out the rest of his life – even performing it in German in Moscow and St Petersburg.

A brilliant comic actor, but a distinctly nervous man – who was plagued by insomnia – Wyndham didn't come into the Garrick quite as regularly as some of his fellow actors, because, as Richard Hough put it in his history: 'He found that, nervous as he was by nature, he would be adding to the trial of his nerves if he partook of supper'. In an effort to tire himself out before retir-ing to bed he would walk from the Club to his home in St John's Wood, but the remedy seldom worked. He nevertheless remained the finest comic actor of his generation – and a member until his death in 1919.

The third great late nineteenth-century portrait of an actor member that hangs in the Cocktail Bar is another full-length oil by Riviere of one of the Club's other luminaries of those days, Sir Squire Bancroft, wearing a long grey frock coat, silk cuffs and a slightly surprised expression. Bancroft joined the Club shortly after Hare, as a young man of twenty-eight in 1869, and remained a member for more than half a century until his death in 1926. Tall, distinguished, as shrewd as he was debonair, he was not, perhaps, quite as talented as Hare or Wyndham, but he was to become one of the great actor-managers, as well as a stalwart of the Garrick, serving on countless committees and as a Trustee. He also found time to produce the plays of two of the Club's members at the Haymarket, *Sweethearts* by Gilbert, and *Lords and Commons* by Pinero.

His loyalty to the Club was matched only by his enthusiasm for funerals. When the death of an elephant at London Zoo was mentioned at lunch one day at the centre table, Gilbert asked: 'Has Bancroft sent a wreath?' In spite of the odd remark, however, 'Old B' was nevertheless held in the highest esteem by his fellow members, as is only too obvious in a Max Beerbohm cartoon entitled *Solemn Scene at the Garrick Club* and dated 1919. Squire Bancroft, complete with monocle, silk hat and fur coat, is addressing his fellow member Gerald Du Maurier. The caption has Bancroft telling him: 'My dear boy, I am just off to Folkestone to join her Ladyship ... I've only five or ten minutes to spare; but I do wish most earnestly to impress on you once more: Hampstead, you know, delightful spot, rural, salubrious, filled with memories of your gifted father – but your position, your leading position in our great profession – how about that. Doesn't it suggest, doesn't it demand for you the lease of a house in – not necessarily Berkeley Square – but somewhere not utterly remote from the home of our Sovereign?'

In fact Bancroft's opinion was widely respected at the Garrick. His only son, who married Sir John Hare's daughter, remembered a lunch at the Club one day when the subject of discussion was the latest controversial production of *Macbeth* with Arthur Bourchier – another member – in the lead role. Well aware that his mother and father had seen the play the day before, the young Bancroft saw his father walk into the Coffee Room and asked him what he thought of the production. There was a long pause while Sir Squire adjusted his eyeglass, before he announced: 'Parts of it were good and parts of it were not so good. The whole question is whether what was good was good enough'. It was a perfect Garrick moment, and a reflection of the importance the Club had developed as a meeting place for the country's leading actors at the dawn of the twentieth century. After the curtain came down some of the greatest talents in British theatre would congregate in the Coffee Room and remain there until well into the small hours – the greatest concentration of theatrical talent anywhere.

The Club possesses a portrait of the last of the great actors and managers to join the Club in Irving's wake, Sir Johnston Forbes-Robertson, who became a member in 1888 at thirty-three, and there is also a striking terracotta bust by Sarah Bobsaris. Sir Johnston's portrait has not so far made it to the heady heights of the Cocktail Bar walls, which is regrettable since his contribution to the Club and the theatre over six decades was certainly a match for his contemporaries who look down from the Bar's walls today.

In his younger days Forbes-Robertson appeared with Irving, Bancroft and Hare, and finally confirmed his reputation in Pinero's *The Profligate* at the Garrick Theatre shortly after the turn of the century when it was under Hare's management. A brilliant Shakespearean, and a supremely graceful actor, his Hamlet was generally regarded as the finest of his time, a fact acknowledged at the annual dinner given in his honour in 1933, four years before his death. The Club's Chairman, Lord Buckmaster, who was also the Lord Chancellor, told the packed Coffee Room audience: 'I like best to think of Forbes-Robertson as a man who helped to reveal to us the wonder and the glory and the power of the greatest Englishman that ever wrote'. He went on to describe his Hamlet, concluding: 'Those who were privileged to see Forbes-Robertson in that part must have gone back to re-read the well-known words with a new light upon their meaning and with a vain effort to recapture the marvellous music of the voice in which the tale had been retold'.

If there was a golden age for actors at the Garrick, it was the era that saw Irving, Tree, Alexander, Hare, Bancroft and Forbes-Robertson among its membership – though there have been, and still are, many fine and enthusiastic actor members to this day. Yet somehow the image of the Coffee Room clouded in smoke, the light from the gas lamps flickering against the pictures, the sound of laughter in the air, brings the Club to life.

9

The Lost Boys

*A*S FOR SO many other British institutions the First World War was the great divide, the moment that brought irreversible changes to the life of this country and its institutions. The Garrick was no exception. The great men who had won it fame during the late Victorian and Edwardian years were growing old. Irving had died nine years before the outbreak of war, Tree was to die within three years of its starting and Sir George Alexander before peace was declared in November 1918. But this is not to imply that the Club was not as harmonious, welcoming and filled with remarkable members as it always had been – just that the great dinosaurs had slowly left the plain.

Not that the lesser lights, stalwarts to a man, were not in evidence. The brilliant cartoonist Linley Sambourne, for example, who had illustrated Charles Kingsley's *The Water Babies* and gone on to become a member of the *Punch* staff, and for the last decade of his life its cartoonist-in-chief, was a familiar member of the '*Punch* table', – the round one at the far left-hand end of the Coffee Room that was to become the publishers' table as the twentieth century progressed. Sambourne was almost as devoted a member as Tree until his death in 1910, while Sir Sidney Low, author and journalist, brilliant editor of the *St James's Gazette* between 1888 and 1897, friend of Cecil Rhodes and Lord Curzon, and an ardent imperialist, who was knighted in 1918, spanned both the Edwardian period and the Great War, remaining a member until his death in 1932.

Two men in particular, however, took up the Irving and Tree standards at the Garrick as Edwardian England came to its end on the fields of Flanders. Pinero and Squire Bancroft soldiered on valiantly, making light of their ever-increasing years, but it was the actor Gerald Du Maurier, who joined in 1903, the year of his marriage, and the creator of *Peter Pan* J.M. Barrie, who were to become the greatest ornaments of the Garrick as the sound of the guns of Picardy echoed on the heights of Hampstead Heath.

Throughout their lives these men seemed to bring out the very best in each other, both on and off the stage. The dashing Du Maurier was one of the few people able to crack the grim, even rather gloomy Barrie façade. One reason was that the unhappily married Barrie was besotted with Du Maurier's elder sister Sylvia, then Mrs Llewelyn Davies, and her five sons. It was those sons, Du Maurier's nephews, that would prompt him to create *Peter Pan*. It was almost inevitable that Du Maurier would appear in the original 1904 production, playing both Captain Hook and Mr Darling.

The son of *Punch* artist and illustrator George Du Maurier, also a member of the Garrick, Gerald Du Maurier was to haunt the Garrick for three decades in the wake of becoming a member in 1903. Slight, with a weak chest from childhood, he was nevertheless charming, utterly engaging, and without a trace of conceit. Peter Pan made his name, but it was playing the cricketing safe-cracker Raffles that made him forever a star just a couple of years later. Du Maurier joined the General Committee just as the Great War broke out and, shortly after the first Zeppelin raid on London on 1 June 1915 he found himself responsible for reviewing the Club's insurance against damage by aircraft. The Committee decided not to take out additional insurance, but they did agree a Roll of Honour should be created in the wake of the fiasco at Gallipoli, and that a major who had been elected but had never had the chance to use the Club before his death should have his entrance fee and first year subscription returned to his family.

Du Maurier and the Committee oversaw a number of cutbacks during the combat. When it was decided that the consumption of electricity had to be substantially reduced, the supply of toast with paté was discontinued. Bread took its place until finally even that was removed, members being left to eat their paté with a knife and fork. But they also introduced a dinner for three shillings and sixpence (17 pence) in an effort to encourage attendance in the evening, while at the same time the Secretary wrote to the staff calling their attention 'to the urgent need of volunteers for the army and navy' and insisting that the Club would keep open the place of every man who joins 'for the duration of the war', as well as making 'an allowance' to their dependants while they were away.

The Committee also decided to amend the rules about blackballing, deciding that when twelve committee members were present, two blackballs would exclude a candidate from membership, while if there were more than twelve Committee members it would require three blackballs – a rule that has remained largely in place. As the twentieth century progressed the arguments over this somewhat arcane procedure were to intensify. The current rule is that if all twenty-four elected members of the General Committee are present at least four blackballs are usually required to exclude a candidate

Nowhere was the Committee's generosity to its fellow members better illuminated than in its sympathetic treatment of Sir Seymour Hicks, who had become a member of the Club in 1899, at twenty-eight, and rapidly established himself as a stalwart – not least in discovering the chair on which Irving died. Hicks was also known for his dry sense of humour in the Club. When asked what he thought of the redecoration to the Garrick's members' lavatory on the ground floor, for example, he famously replied: 'Oh quite all right dear boy. The only trouble is that it makes my cock look so shabby'. That at least is the legend, although many other members have claimed the joke.

Equally renowned for the gardenia he perpetually wore in his buttonhole, a mounted prop version of which sits in the show-case on the first-floor landing, the outbreak of war had thrown the actor-manager on distinctly hard times – so hard, in fact, that he was (to his intense embarrassment) forced to the very brink of bankruptcy. It was a disgrace that could not permit him to remain a member of the Club. But, and it is a significant but, though a Petition for Bankruptcy had been issued in December 1914, no proceedings had actually been taken. By May 1915, however, Hicks had accepted the inevitable and wrote to the Secretary say-ing: 'I must to my deep regret cease to be a member of the most delightful Club in London. Perhaps one day I shall be re-selected. I hope so very sincerely'. But the Committee was not minded to lose so distinguished and enthusiastic a member quite so easily. After a considerable amount of thought one Committee member at the time was designated to tell Hicks that as he had not actu-ally been adjudicated a bankrupt he could withdraw his resigna-tion. Vastly relieved, Hicks did so without delay.

But there were also some good moments during the war years. In 1916 Sir Francis Burnand, an enthusiastic member since 1865 and editor of *Punch* for what seemed almost as long, was elected a Life Member, and a year later a gift of a silver salver was gratefully accepted from Lady Tree in the wake of her late husband's death. (Queen Victoria had presented the salver to Tree in 1894.) At the same time the Club elected members who would become its lifeblood in the years to come. Alfred Duff Cooper was elected in 1917: 'I felt proud, romantic and exalted', he wrote to his wife Diana. Shortly afterwards so was the Jersey-born son of a seaman Freddy Lonsdale, whose drawing-room comedies, notably *The Last of Mrs Cheyney*, were to illuminate the English theatre of the 1920s.

The ghost of Sir Henry Irving still stalked the Club's cor-ridors, if not literally then certainly metaphorically. In 1918 the Committee elected his artist grandson Laurence to membership at the astonishingly young age of twenty. The Committee made an exception not just because of his ancestry, but also because his father had drowned after a U-boat attack on the ship in which he was travelling. A year later, in May 1919, the death of Laurence's uncle – Irving's younger son – also called Henry was announced on the notice board. He was just forty-nine, and had made his acting debut in 1891 under Sir John Hare. The Club sent a letter of condolence and flowers to his widow Dorothea Baird, who had enjoyed her first stage success as Trilby opposite Tree's Svengali.

When he was elected to the Club at the age of thirty, in 1890, James Matthew Barrie was exultant. 'There will be joy in the Garrick', he wrote to a friend when he heard he had been elected, 'when I burst upon it like a sunbeam' – a rather unexpected remark for a man who could certainly seem a shade less than sunny, even dour, to those who did not know him well. To be fair, Barrie could also appear dismissive, even to his fellow members, and one of his biographers, Dennis Mackail, noted: 'At the Garrick when actors talked J.M.B. had a mild impulse to listen, if not to join in, and an impulse more than mild when the talker was Henry Irving, the one actor of all actors Barrie could never pretend to despise'.

The son of a handloom weaver, who studied at the University of Edinburgh, Barrie served for two years as a journalist in Nottinghamshire before coming to London to try his hand as a freelance writer in 1885. His first successful book was *Auld Licht Idylls*, published in 1888, sketches of life in his native Kirriemuir, Scotland. His second novel, *The Little Minister*, published shortly after he became a member of the Garrick, was a considerable success, and within six years had been turned into an equally successful play. From then on a significant proportion of Barrie's work was for the theatre, notably *The Admirable Crichton* of 1902.

Deeply attached to his mother, Barrie even made her the heroine of his novel *Margaret Ogilvy* of 1896, but his relationship with his wife, the actress Mary Ansell whom he married in 1894, was far less satisfactory – 'childless and apparently unconsummated', according to the *Encyclopaedia Britannica*. Nevertheless Barrie found consolation with Arthur and Sylvia Llewelyn Davies – Mrs Llewelyn Davies was Gerald Du Maurier's elder sister –

and their five sons, to whom he told the stories that were to become the basis of the play *Peter Pan*, first performed in London in 1904.

Like so many stories of Garrick members, however, success is all too often tinged with tragedy. Barrie divorced Mary Ansell in April 1910, three years after Sylvia Llewelyn Davies had become a widow. Tragically she was to die herself just four months later, leaving Barrie to act as guardian to her sons. One of them, George, was killed in the trenches, while another, the gifted Michael – often said to be the model for Peter Pan – died in a freak accident while bathing as an Oxford undergraduate shortly after the end of the war. The deaths seemed to confirm for ever Barrie's disenchantment with adult life, a view that was reflected in his finest play, *Dear Brutus*, first performed in 1917, where nine men and women whose lives have come to grief are given a mysterious 'second chance' only to be wrecked again on the reefs of their own temperaments.

But Barrie's disenchantment with adults did not extend to the Garrick nor to its members. Indeed, his friend and fellow member, Gerald Du Maurier, played the Honourable Ernest Woolley in the 326 performances of the original production of *The Admirable Crichton* at the Duke of York's, as well as in the 1908 revival. Both productions being directed by fellow Garrick member Dion Boucicault. As Guy Boas memorably put it in his history of the Club of 1948: 'Gerald was the perfect Barrie actor, and Barrie the perfect Du Maurier dramatist' – not least in performing the role of Dearth in *Dear Brutus*. Du Maurier even presented the play, having taken control of the Wyndham's Theatre, along with Frank Curzon, in 1910, where it had its premiere in 1917.

Barrie was not, however, the only writer of substance in the Club as the Great War finally came to its end. Another was Kenneth Grahame, a Scot who became Secretary to the Bank of England, but is far better remembered for a book that he never intended to be published, which was based on bedtime stories for his son. The manuscript of Grahame's tale of the riverbank, *The Wind in the Willows*, was given reluctantly to an impoverished

American publisher, who subsequently rejected it. And even when it first appeared in 1908, its reception was muted. It was to be some years before the story of Mole, Rat, Badger, and, of course, Toad, was to become established as a children's classic. Indeed its final acclamation was to wait until its dramatisation by a fellow member, one A.A. Milne, in 1929, of whom we shall hear more.

THE GARRICK CLUB

Keen, Benjamin, Esq., Barrister

An old schoolfellow of mine and a clever writer. He was at one time connected with the *Morning Chronicle* and *Globe*, but afterwards had a good practice at the Chancery Bar.

Kemble, Charles, Esq., F.S.A.

The celebrated tragedian, brother of John Philip Kemble, and father of Fanny Kemble, afterwards Mrs. Butler. A member of the Committee. On retiring from the stage he succeeded George Colman as Dramatic Licenser, and lived in Park Place, St. James's, in very good society, where I often dined with him.

Knowles, James Sheridan, Esq.

The author and actor. He was admitted an honorary member on the success of his play "The Hunchback."

Laporte, Peter Francis, Esq.

Manager of the Opera House.

36

10

Maugham and Milne

N O ONE could deny that the world was a different place in the wake of the Great War, and no one could be more aware of that than the members of the Garrick. There was hardly a member who had not lost a relative in the trenches, and hardly a member who did not feel that loss as an almost physical pain.

The Club had also lost one of its luminaries, though not on the battlefield, with the death of Sir Herbert Beerbohm Tree in 1917. But just a few months after the armistice was signed, Tree was to return to the Club, at least on canvas, when his executors agreed to sell the Honourable John Collier's magnificent painting of Tree, Ellen Terry and Madge Kendall in *The Merry Wives of Windsor*. The Club paid the sum of one hundred guineas, having persuaded 100 members to contribute one guinea each to secure it.

The painting now hangs in what has become known as the Milne Room but in those days was simply the Smoking room, where members could be found after lunch sleeping gently in its leather armchairs. After the works by Zoffany in the Coffee Room, and the great Clint in the hall, it remains a favourite among the Club's finest paintings, not least for the sense of mischief twinkling in the eyes of both actresses just before they bundle the slightly stunned Tree into the basket to be carried out by the servants and dumped in the middy ditch at Datchet Mead on the Thames.

There were other, equally touching, bequests in the days after the war. In July 1919, for example, Lady Edward Cecil, who was to go on to become editor of the *National Review*, wrote to say that in 1915, shortly before her son Edward had been sent to France with the Grenadiers, he had 'bought an old theatre programme – about 100 years old – to give to the Garrick'. But then 'he was seized with shyness and thought it was not worthy perhaps – adding "I'll give it when I come back"'. He never did, and died – as his mother so poignantly puts it – 'amidst the beech woods of Villers-Cotterets'. 'Would the Garrick accept this trifle from my dear boy who owed so much gratitude to you and to so many members of the Garrick for their kindness to him?' The programme remains in the Library still, as does the signed copy of George Meredith's novel *Beauchamp's Career* that Lady Edward Cecil gave at the same time. Times were changing, and in 1919, Henry B. Irving, son of the great actor died, removing the last but one Irving link with the Club.

Despite these great losses, the Garrick gradually gathered itself, and the sound of laughter rather than tears started to echo once more in the Coffee Room. On 16 September 1921 the Club played host to a remarkable dinner for the newly famous star of the silent screen Charlie Chaplin, who was paying a visit to his native London in the wake of his extraordinary success. At dinner Chaplin sat next to Barrie, who suggested that he should play Peter Pan. Legend has it that Chaplin was deeply shocked at the idea, and rapidly changed the subject, though Barrie was convinced that he had taken the idea seriously.

In fact Chaplin didn't much care for the Club, describing its atmosphere as 'chiaroscuro' and relating in his autobiography forty years later that, apart from Barrie, he had also met Edwin Lutyens and Squire Bancroft. 'But I felt the evening didn't quite come off … During dinner, Frampton, the sculptor, attempted levity and was charming, but he had difficulty scintillating in the gloom of the Garrick Club.' Chaplin was not alone in finding the

Sir Squire Bancroft by Hugh Goldwin Riviere
(Cat. G0028)

Sir Gerald Du Maurier by Sir Bernard Partridge
(Cat. G0174)

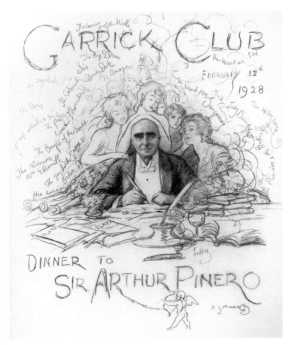

Sir Arthur Wing Pinero by Sir Alfred Munnings
(Cat. G0671)

Sir Alfred Munnings by John Gilroy
(Cat. G0631)

Christopher Robin Milne by E.H. Shepard
(Cat. G0608)

A.A. Milne by Sir David Low (Cat. G1013)

Arthur Ransome by John Gilroy (Cat. G0711)

Derby Day by John Gilroy (Cat. G892)

Sir Noël Coward by Edward Seago (Cat. G0139)

Sir Laurence Olivier by Bernard Hailstone (Cat. G0642)

Frederick Barker by
John Gilroy (Cat. G0043)

Lord Charles Russell by
John Gilroy (Cat. G0728)

Sir John Gielgud by David Remfry (Cat. G0969)

Sir Donald Sinden by Clive Francis (Cat. 0981)

Club difficult in those post-war years. Five years after his visit the playwright Sean O'Casey found it every bit as unappetising. But for every unhappy visitor there were more than a handful of far happier members.

The actor Sir Johnston Forbes-Robertson, grand-uncle of one of the Club's current members, Dominick Harrod, was as enthusiastic and committed as ever. A member since 1888, he had become as much of a stalwart as Squire Bancroft – by now one of the three Trustees – and Seymour Hicks, and his portrait by George Harcourt hangs in the Irving Room, just as his bust by Sarah Bobsaris now stands sentinel at the entrance to the Cocktail Bar. Every bit an eminent Victorian, tall, strikingly gaunt, and with a penchant for morning coats, Forbes-Robertson was described by one of his fellow members as 'a man of distinction and great charm, whose performances in romantic parts carried away his audiences, illustrated and expounded as they were by one of the most beautiful speaking voices we have had on the stage'. He was to remain a devoted member throughout the next two decades, until his death, at the age of eighty-six, in 1939.

Another of the actor members in the twenties was A.E. 'Matty' Matthews, kindly, sensitive, but also 'lovable and mischievous', according to one of his contemporaries. Matthews, like one or two of his fellow actors at the time, favoured a rather distinctive menu when eating, which involved drinking cocoa with his main course and concluding with crème de menthe, occasionally followed by 'Gentleman's Relish' on toast. But he loved the Club with a passion.

Sir John Gielgud vividly recalled working with him between the wars. They got on very well during rehearsals, and when they met once – by accident – in the street, Gielgud happened to ask Matthews where he was going. 'To the Garrick Club', came the reply. 'And then, quick as a flash' Gielgud remembered, 'seeing by the look in my eye that I was not yet a member of that august fellowship, added, "I like the lavatories there so much. They have handles at the sides that help you to pull yourself up".' Gielgud did not become a member himself for another three decades.

But as the affluence of the twenties began to sweep through

the Club, so the literary members came to outshine even the most glamorous of their acting contemporaries. The most distinguished author of the period, though not perhaps the most clubbable, was Somerset Maugham, born in Paris in 1874, the fourth surviving son of a lawyer attached to the British Embassy. His mother died when he was eight, and his father just two years later, and the young William was sent to live with a childless middle-aged aunt and clergyman uncle in Whitstable, Kent. Educated at King's School, Canterbury, and Heidelberg University, he went on to study medicine at St Thomas's Hospital – drawing on his experiences as an obstetric clerk for his first novel, *Liza of Lambeth*, in 1897. A disciplined, even workaholic, writer, he produced prodigious numbers of novels and plays.

A distinctly reserved, though never conventional, man, handicapped by a severe stammer, Maugham was not an overnight success, but by 1908 had the distinction of having no fewer than four plays running at the same time in the West End – a feat that a later member, Terence Rattigan, did everything he could to equal, but only ever in fact managing three. In 1911 Maugham met Syrie Wellcome, daughter of the famous Dr Barnardo, then the wife of an American businessman. Maugham and Syrie had a daughter, inevitably called Liza, in 1915, and finally married in 1917.

In 1914, while working for an ambulance unit in Flanders, Maugham met Gerald Haxton, a young man eighteen years his junior who was rapidly to become his secretary and permanent companion. Within two years the two had set out on the first of many journeys to the Far East, experiences that would appear throughout his short stories. It was when he returned to Britain after one of these trips that he was first elected a member of the Garrick – which he regarded as a great honour. Indeed he would continue to arrive to play bridge once or twice a week when he was in England and not at the Villa Mauresque, his house at Cap Ferrat, until the last year of his life in 1965.

If Maugham was the most distinguished writer, another, whom he supported for membership, was to play a decisive role in securing the future of the Club: A.A. (Alan Alexander) Milne, always known as 'Blue' to his friends and family. Born in 1892 and educated at Westminster and Trinity College, Cambridge, he came to the Garrick through the *Punch* route. He had become assistant editor of the magazine in 1906, a job he had held until 1914. He was elected shortly after his war service, in March 1919, and was to remain an enthusiastic, not to say dedicated member, until his death in 1956 at the age of sixty-eight. Originally elected as an 'author, journalist, dramatist', it was Milne's plays that first made his reputation, as well as a remarkable detective novel, *The Red House*, published in 1922, which one critic called 'the most entertaining book of its kind written during the twenties.'

Milne's plays, which included *Mr Pim Passes By* of 1920, *The Dover Road* of 1922 and *To Have the Honour* of 1924, usually featured some of his fellow Garrick members, including Allan Aynesworth and Gerald Du Maurier, achieving respectable, if not exactly long, runs in the West End. And in 1929 he dramatised his fellow member Kenneth Grahame's *The Wind in the Willows* – the only one of his plays that was to survive in print long after his death. But it was his book of children's verses, *When We Were Very Young* of 1924, followed by the phenomenally successful *Winnie-the-Pooh* just two years later that were to transform his life, his reputation, and his – and the Garrick's – financial position. The equally successful *The House at Pooh Corner* followed it up in 1928. Illustrated by another member, and *Punch* hand, Ernest Shepard, the books were to become, and remain, worldwide bestsellers.

It was Milne's devotion to the Club that was to see him leave one quarter of the earnings of his children's books – the so-called Pooh royalties – to the Garrick following his death in 1956. It was first estimated that these would bring in some £40,000 per annum. The reality is that they brought in far more, literally millions of pounds, first in royalties and then in a lump sum payment from the Disney corporation that capitalised the remaining years of royalty income and saw the Garrick receive a sum of almost £40m. Ironically, Milne and his family had long been convinced that it would be his plays that would ensure his fame and fortune. In his autobiography he even wrote: 'I am not inordinately fond of or interested in children. I intend to escape from them'. In recognition of his generosity, which exceeded even Pinero's in 1934, the Club decided to name a room in his memory, an honour only later extended to Irving.

Milne was to remain one of the staunchest members of the Garrick throughout the interwar period, spanning the passing of the last of the Edwardians, like Pinero, and the newer breed, including P.G. Wodehouse, who had been elected shortly after Milne. By then in his early forties, Wodehouse too came to the Club through the *Punch* connection, having established himself as one of the magazine's most widely read humorists, a talent he also displayed to great effect in *Strand Magazine*. This Guildford-born son of a civil servant published the first of his 120 novels in 1902, and in 1917 produced *The Man with Two Left Feet*, which introduced the characters of Jeeves and Wooster to the world. In the decade that followed, Wodehouse brought out some of his finest comic novels featuring the two, as well as Lord Emsworth and his prize sow the Empress of Blandings, a myriad of aunts and, of course, the members of the Drones Club.

In 1927 one member sat next to Wodehouse at dinner and recalled: 'During my hasty meal I sat next to a man I thought charming. He was both humble and shy. We discovered we had both been to America and discussed the country. Because he was humble I became patronising, and when I left I casually asked the headwaiter who the gentleman was I had been sitting next to – "Mr P.G. Wodehouse". I wished I'd been nicer'. When Wodehouse was captured at Le Touquet at the start of the Second World War, the Germans encouraged him to broadcast to the Americans. The broadcast caused a scandal in England, but not amongst the members of the Club. Wodehouse eventually resigned his membership and settled in the United States until his death in 1975 at the age of ninety-four.

If Maugham was the most successful member, another of his contemporaries could certainly claim greater distinction. Herbert George Wells was sixty-six when he finally became a member of the Club in 1932. The son of an unsuccessful tradesman who was also a professional cricketer, he was eight years older than Maugham, but achieved his first success at almost exactly the same time as his more precocious contemporary, with the publication of what could justifiably claim to be the first 'science fiction' novel, *The Time Machine*, in 1895. He was certainly every bit as unconventional as Maugham. After struggling as a teacher – writing in his spare time – he married his cousin Isabel only to elope with a student, Catherine 'Jane' Robbins, within a matter of months (though this did nothing to prevent his embarking on a string of other relationships and criticising so-called 'conventional' marriage).

Wells's literary output was vast, ranging from science fiction to romance, from *The Island of Doctor Moreau* and *The Invisible Man* to *Kipps* and *The History of Mr Polly*, which recounts the adventures of an inefficient shopkeeper who liberates himself by burning down his own shop and retreating to the Potwell Inn. Wells's one experiment in autobiography, published just two years after he became a member of the Club, provides a string of striking portraits of his contemporaries, including Arnold Bennett, who happened to live in the same block of flats in Baker Street as Wells himself.

One other key literary member in these interwar years was A.E.W. Mason, author of the patriotic 1902 story *The Four Feathers* evoking Harry Feversham's heroism in redeeming himself from accusations of cowardice in the eyes of his three fellow officers and his beloved Ethne Eustace. A former actor who turned to writing in despair at his lack of success on the stage, Mason later created French detective Inspector Hanaud in a crime series that began with *At The Villa Rose* in 1910. Gentle, eloquent and famous for his dry sense of humour, he was to remain a member until his death in 1948.

But the writers were not the main force at the single most glittering event in the Club's history – the Centenary Dinner on 22 November 1931. That honour fell to the lawyers, and retired lawyers, who made up almost half the 152 members who attended that evening. The leather-bound book containing the signatures of all the members who attended is still in the Club's library, as indeed is the bound programme for the very first anniversary dinner held on 15 February 1832 with the Duke of Sussex in the chair. The king's son was not in the chair for the Centenary Dinner, but the Prince of Wales, who was, however briefly, to become King Edward VIII within a matter of years, was certainly sitting at the top table on that Sunday evening in 1931. He was seated alongside the Chairman, and one of the Club's Trustees, Stanley Owen Buckmaster, the first Viscount Buckmaster, who was then seventy and had been Lord Chancellor from 1915 until 1916.

The top table was crowded with the Club's senior members. Alfred Munnings RA, later to become President of the Royal Academy, and a member since 1922, sat beside fellow artist Sir Edwin Lutyens, RA, a member since 1916. Also at the table was Seymour Hicks, who had been a member of the Club since 1899, then still to be knighted, even though he had built the Aldwych Theatre. Maurice Codner's portrait of Hicks in white tie for his role as Lucien in his own adaptation of the French play *The Man in Dress Clothes* hangs in the Cocktail Bar.

Buckmaster's speech to the assembled company contains the single most eloquent description of membership that has ever been formulated, and one that holds as true today as it did then. This 'beautifully equipped judge', in the words of one his successors as Lord Chancellor, told the hushed Coffee Room that evening, with the guests from the Strangers' Dining Room – now the Irving Room – standing along the walls: 'There is one thing about this Club which we all prize. It makes no difference from where they come, it makes no difference what members do, it does not make much difference, within reasonable limits, what they say'. At this point legend has it there was some gentle laughter and the Chairman paused. But then he continued: 'Old and young, wise and foolish, can all meet together on terms of common equality. Men are measured here not judged on achievement, or rank, or wealth, or fame, or power; they are judged on merits of gaiety and companionship; and upon that platform old and young can join hands'. As he sat down the applause was thunderous.

One of the junior lawyers whose signature appears in the volume that commemorates the Centenary Dinner belonged to a twenty-nine-year-old barrister who had been elected just a few months earlier. His name was Melford Stevenson and he would go on to become a mainstay of the Garrick over the next fifty-six years. Just four years later he was joined by an even younger businessman named Nicholas Harris, who remains the father of the Club to this day: our longest surviving member. Both were to see the Club struggle in the decades to come, grappling with first another war and then the austerities that followed.

Sir Henry Irving by Sir Frank Lockwood
'Henry meets his first pheasant.'
Presented by HM King George V, 1930

11

Hard Times

A S THE threat of war stalked Europe for the second time in
barely a generation, so the Garrick began to recognise that it
was on the brink of another very different world. The magnificent pictures still stared down from the walls. Nell Gwyn still
smiled enigmatically, as did Peg Woffington, Colley Cibber and
Charles Kemble, recently joined by a caricature of Irving by Sir
Frank Lockwood, presented by King George V. The silver snuff
boxes that sat along the centre table were still there, as were the
candelabra, and even the original 'Gin Punch', taken with iced
soda water, was still consumed on special occasions. But the world
was beginning to move ever more rapidly in a disturbing direction.

By February 1939 the Picture Committee, as the Works of
Art Committee was then known, presided over by Sir Alfred
Munnings, had decided that it was going to remove all the
Zoffanys 'in the event of a War emergency'. They also decided
that as many of the other pictures as possible should be put into
the cellar and the outside wall sandbagged. Two months later
they ordered wooden cases, and asked the General Committee to
decide when the pictures should be removed. On Tuesday
5 September 1938 eight cases were packed and taken to

Chadlington in Oxfordshire, later to be moved to Newport Pagnell, while a further two wooden cases – containing the best of the Zoffanys – went to the cellars of Shell Mex House three days later.

As the war began and the air raid sirens started to wail nightly over London so the Garrick was transformed, at least to look at, but the members remained utterly unmoved. Indeed the membership expanded steadily throughout the Blitz, which left the Club shaken but thankfully not stirred, and the actors remained some of its firmest supporters. One of this band was Allan Aynesworth, who had joined the Club in 1895 at the age of just thirty and was to remain a member for an astonishing sixty-one years; just before the outbreak of war he was joined by the gentle Felix Aylmer, and the strikingly handsome Leslie Howard. Portraits of all three remain in the Cocktail Bar to this day.

Tragically, Howard was to become one of the Club's handful of fatalities in the conflict. Another was Flight Lieutenant Richard Hillary, who recovered from the terrible burns he suffered during the Battle of Britain only to be killed flying on the very night he was elected a member. His name and Howard's are among the eight on the entrance hall plaque that commemorates the dead of both wars.

The war also saw the election of musicians Arthur Bliss and William Walton, as well as playwright Kenneth Horne, but it was three other actor members who were particularly to distinguish themselves and the Garrick in the years to come. In 1942 Donald Wolfit – the knighthood was to come later – joined the Club, to be followed the next year by Alistair Sim and John Clements, whose portraits remain in the Bar still, though Wolfit's has moved. The magnificent Sim, star of so many of Britain's best film comedies, was a keen bridge player, though his colleagues privately chided him for 'always revealing what was in his hand by the size of the smile on his face'. The more reserved Clements, founder not only of the Chichester Festival Theatre but also the Intimate Theatre, Palmer's Green, was every bit as enthusiastic a member, repairing to the Club after stage performances, no matter what the V1 or V2 flying bombs might threaten.

But the new actor member who was to make the most impact was Wolfit, born Don Woolfitt in Nottinghamshire in 1902, who had made his first appearance on the London stage in 1924 alongside Matheson Lang in *The Wandering Jew*. Wolfit, as he rechristened himself, was one of the London stage's greatest ornaments throughout the war, performing at lunchtime at the Strand Theatre when the Blitz made evening performances impossible, and then at 6pm when the bombing relented a little. As a current member, Sir Michael Davies, has written in the Club newsletter *The Garrick*: 'Those who saw his Lear, his Hamlet, his Shylock – not forgetting his Volpone – and other great performances, sometimes two or three different long roles in the same week, will ever remember them'.

Forever to be seen sporting the Garrick Club tie, Wolfit was to become one of the most devoted and popular members of the Garrick – even though he was not so universally liked or admired by his contemporaries, be they actors or critics. 'It was a place with magic in it', he would often repeat. Always known as 'Sir' by the members of his company, this last great actor-manager was immortalised in current Garrick member Ronald Harwood's play and later film *The Dresser* – Harwood acted as Wolfit's dresser and business manager in the actor's later years – the part of Wolfit was played in the theatre by another actor member, Freddie Jones, while the part of the dresser was played on stage and screen by yet another current member, Sir Tom Courtney. Wolfit seemed to seep into every pore of the Club, remaining there in spirit until long after his death in 1968, at the age of only sixty-two. Never quite the match for Irving, he was nevertheless one actor whose personality seemed to dominate the place, not least the Coffee Room, where he would sometimes rise from his seat and give a low bow if a particularly distinguished judge were to pass him.

Apart from the arrival of a new generation of actors, there were other harbingers of changing times. In December 1941, for example, the General Committee amended one of the Club's by-laws to the effect that 'Ladies may be brought to luncheon on Sundays at the side tables'. It was the first time that women had been admitted through the Garrick's portals. With women in uniform crowding the streets of London, there were members who thought this was the thin end of the wedge and that women would soon overrun the Club. But they need not have feared – indeed it would be another half century before the issue of whether they might become members was even debated.

The appearance of ladies on a Sunday didn't appear to ruffle the male members unduly. And the newer actors suddenly found themselves joined by a journalist-turned-author who was to make a distinctive impression on the Club. Arthur Michell Ransome, the Leeds-born son of a professor of history, had been educated at Rugby and gone on to become a reporter on the *Daily News*. In 1913 he sent himself to Russia to learn the language, and ended up covering the Russian Revolution for the paper. The experiences were to inspire his first book, *Old Peter's Russian Tales*, which was a considerable success. In 1924, at the age of forty, he married for a second time; his bride was Evgenia Shelepin, who had been Trotsky's secretary. Six year later, he published the first of a series of children's books that were to make his name: *Swallows and Amazons*.

The stories of the Walker and Blackett families, as well as their friends, in locations from the Lake District to the Norfolk Broads were to continue for seventeen years, until the publication of the last volume, *Great Northern*, in 1947. By that time, however, Ransome had established himself as a formidable new member of the Garrick, joining just months after Alistair Sim. John Gilroy's admirable portrait of this slightly stiff, but affectionate man, who was a keen fly-fisherman, hangs across the Bar from Edward Seago's portrait of Sim. It precisely captures Ransome's watchful strength, for he was not a man to be trifled with. When one current member, then very new, was introduced to him under the stairs in his later years, he made the mistake of saying 'You're not THE Arthur Ransome are you?' The author looked across the top of his glasses and said firmly: 'Is there another one?'

A fearsome bridge player, who also liked to play billiards, Ransome haunted the Club throughout the war, often playing cards past midnight, along with Sim and others. On such occasions they were attended by one member of the staff who was to become a legend all of his own. Frederick Barker, always known as Freddy, who had taken charge of wine in the Coffee Room in 1936, was to become one of the Club's finest, if least likely, adornments over the next three decades.

When the members played bridge late into the night, it was usually Barker who stayed to supply them with whatever they required after the rest of the staff had disappeared. Ever grave, and supremely diplomatic, Barker would suggest to the bridge players, as midnight approached, that perhaps this might be the last rubber. 'Oh just another one Barker, and a round.' Barker would disappear obediently and return with a tray of drinks. So grateful were the bridge players that they would offer to pay for his taxi home, and Barker would solemnly thank them for their generosity – and generous it was for he lived just round the corner in Long Acre and could walk there easily in a matter of minutes. Both members and Barker knew the other knew – but both, in the finest Garrick tradition, declined to notice.

Barker was famously welcoming to members' children, many of whom went on to become members themselves and still recall him getting them their first glass of lemonade when they were invited to the Club by their fathers. But it was not only his kindness that stuck in their minds, it was also his ability to destroy the English language with a skill Mrs Malaprop might have admired. Standing discreetly at the door watching the Queen's arrival for the State Opening of Parliament on the recently acquired Reading Room television set in his later years, for example, Barker was asked, 'What did you like best about it?'. Without a moment's hesitation he replied: 'Oh, it was lovely, sir. It was the indignity of it I liked best'. An overseas member, who came to the Garrick rarely, was delighted to be greeted by name by Barker as he opened the swing door for him at the top of the stairs. 'Tell me, Barker', the delighted member asked, 'how is it that you manage to remember the names of members you haven't seen for years?' Again Barker replied without a pause: 'Well, sir, you see we try and pick on some redeeming feature'.

So significant was Barker to become in his later years that the conductor Sir Malcolm Sargent, who was a member of the Club from 1927 until his death half a century later, launched the 'Barker Club', which had its own visitors' book, to be signed by all those members and guests who had visited what became known as Barker's Arms, the Dispense Bar, after working hours. When it was finally presented to the Garrick after Barker's retirement – it is now in the Library – it was found to contain the signatures of Her Majesty Queen Elizabeth the Queen Mother, their Royal Highnesses Princess Margaret and Princess Anne, Earl Mountbatten of Burma, Lord Alexander of Tunis and Field Marshall Sir Claude Auchinleck, among many others. John Gilroy's painting of Barker hangs above the door of the Cocktail Bar, evidence, if ever any were needed, of the quite astonishing affection in which the members held him.

Unlikely though it may sound today, the wartime Garrick was also home to one or two Labour politicians, notably Ernest Bevin, Minister of Labour in Churchill's government, who became a member of the Club shortly after becoming a member of the War Cabinet. Bevin liked to dine at the members' table, and one evening encountered an elderly fellow member who only rarely visited the Club seated beside him. The elderly member failed to recognise Bevin's Somerset accent, just as he failed to recognise Bevin, and said suddenly: 'I think your President has done a wonderful job'. 'What do you mean, my President', Bevin said, clearly perplexed. 'Aren't you an American?', replied the elderly member. 'No I am not', Bevin answered. 'You must excuse me', he was told, 'I very seldom come here, could you tell me your name?' 'My name is Bevin.' 'How interesting', said the elderly member, 'what do you do for a living?' The formidable Bevin dined out on the story for years.

Bevin wasn't the only Socialist MP to be elected to the Garrick, however; another was Dick Stokes, proposed by Ashley Dukes. Not that the proposer was too certain that his candidate would actually make it past the General Committee. Indeed he was so relieved when Stokes was elected that he sent him a telegram: 'Along the wires the electric message ran: They did not nigro-globulate our man' – clearly to have said 'blackball' would not have been in the spirit of the Garrick. The Club had not always been so forgiving. In 1924 Seymour Hicks blackballed Lewis Casson, remarking: 'We're not going to have any bloody Socialists in the Garrick'. But two decades later the General Committee, at the instigation of the then elderly Hicks, asked Casson if he would like to join. When the two men met Casson feigned indecision, saying 'I'll think about it Seymour'. But join he did, and came for lunch on Tuesdays until his late eighties, to the joy of his remarkable wife, Dame Sybil Thorndike.

But as victory in Europe was followed by victory in Japan, the euphoria that gripped the nation did not last long, and the austerity that followed hit the Garrick with every bit as much severity as it hit the rest of Britain. The paintings were gradually restored to their rightful place on the walls, and the sticky tape removed from the outside walls. In October 1946 the General Committee decided to allow ladies the use of the Morning Room until 3pm on Sundays as they needed 'a more suitable room to sit in'. The wine still flowed, dispensed by the irreplaceable Barker, but the food was another matter entirely. The luncheon menu for 24 January 1948, for example, included the following information: 'The maximum permitted by Food (Restriction on Meals in Establishments) Order 1941 is: (a) One main dish and one subsidiary dish, or (b) Two subsidiary dishes. Soups, vegetarian dishes and sweets may be ordered in addition'. The subsidiary dishes were grilled sausages with onion sauce: price two shillings, served hot; luncheon sausage at one shilling, and liver sausage at one shilling and sixpence, served cold. The 'unrationed' dishes were tomato omelette at two shillings and soused herring at nine pence.

Perhaps it was the food, or the memory of the carnage that had just come to an end, but in the wake of the Second World War a rather unseemly row broke out in the Garrick – one that threatened its tradition of good fellowship. On 26 February 1948 Robert Lutyens, son of Sir Edwin, launched into a discussion of the new exhibition of Chagall paintings at the Tate Gallery with two of his fellow members, Sir Alfred Munnings, then President of the Royal Academy, and *The Times* typographer Stanley Morison, a conscientious objector during the First World War who had been an esteemed member since 1931 and had been editor of the *Times Literary Supplement* from 1945 to 1947. Lutyens praised the exhibition, and this infuriated Munnings, who launched into a tirade. The tirade included what Lutyens, in a letter to the Chairman three days later, called 'violent abuse of the Curator of the Tate Gallery Mr John Rothenstein, saying that "he was a bloody Jew, which was why he showed pictures of another one"'.

Lutyens was shocked, and protested, as did Morison, but that only inflamed Munnings even more. As Lutyens recounted in his letter to the Chairman, Munnings went on to inform 'all who cared to listen and Mr Morison in particular, that here was I expressing these opinions, whereas my grandfather had been a "real" painter – he painted horses – and my father was a great architect – that he had built cathedrals and bridges; whereas, he shouted at me, "you have built neither cathedrals nor bridges". "Why!" he exclaimed, "You're not even an architect"'. They were harsh words to throw at a man who was actually a Fellow of the Royal Institute of British Architects.

The Chairman asked Munnings for an explanation. The great man wrote back, unabashed, and unwilling to apologise: 'When such a sour fellow tells the President of the Royal Academy, in the most traditional Club in London, that Chagall is a great artist and that those who cannot understand him have no idea of art, what is he to do?'. Wisely, the General Committee backed away from taking sides in the dispute, saying only that it 'did not intend to pursue the matter any further' after hearing Sir Alfred's explanation of his actions. Gradually the atmosphere lightened, and Robert Lutyens went on to paint Stanley Morison's portrait, a sketch for which is still in the Club's possession.

In fact, the early months of 1948 were tumultuous for the Garrick. Earlier in February, the Chief Metropolitan Magistrate, Sir Bertrand Watson, died in the Club at lunch. The sixty-nine-year-old former mayor of his native town of Stockton-on-Tees, and its MP from 1917 to 1923 had come to the Club straight from hearing cases at Bow Street and collapsed in the Coffee

Room. But later that year the Club's second history, written by the estimable Guy Boas, a successor to Percy Fitzgerald's 1904 discursive version, was published. The *Sunday Times* called it a 'concise and deftly amusing narrative' that preserved the rumours and the repartee.

Ladies, meanwhile, steadily continued their advance. In June 1950 they were allowed to use the Morning Room any time they happened to be a guest of a member holding a party in the Private Dining Room, provided that they used the small staircase. Within two years they were allowed to dine on Mondays, Tuesdays and Wednesdays 'as an experiment for six months'. One reason was that very few members dined in the Club on those evenings, and the Garrick's finances were suffering. By the spring of 1954 things were very bad indeed. The Club recorded a loss for Coronation Year of £7,300, and the membership had fallen from 597 to 588. The Chairman reported gloomily that they were suffering the effects of rising wages for the staff.

The Club's response was to sell £2,000 worth of Defence Bonds, increase the mortgage on its premises from £20,000 to £30,000 and raise the subscription from £21 to £26.25 a year. But the General Committee also took a decision that was fundamentally to alter the way in which the Club operated. At the Annual General Meeting on 26 April 1954, they recommended to the members that the Garrick should have a bar – until that moment one had never existed, and whatever drinks a member required were produced from the Dispense Bar and delivered to whatever room the member was in. The meeting was heated, one elderly member insisting that he would never use it, but then admitting that if the younger members wanted one it would be churlish to refuse. They did, and so did the Committee, and a bar was duly agreed to. It started life in what had been the Library, directly opposite the top of the main stairs, and is now known as the Reading Room. The card players moved next door, into what, ironically, was eventually to become the Cocktail Bar.

In fact there had been experiments with a bar of sorts the year before in what is now called the Old Card Room, down the coat corridor and past the lavatory. Bottles were spread out on a table and one of the Club's waiters, 'a man called Last' according to one of our current members, former barrister Gerard Noel, 'would stand to dispense drinks'. Unfortunately the said Last didn't seem capable of keeping his own hands off the bottles, and, after being found 'hopelessly drunk on several occasions', his services were dispensed with. But the new Bar, set up in the right-hand corner of the room as you went in, was an immediate success, soon to be presided over by the inimitable Tony Wilde, with his elephantine memory for names, who was to become an institution at the Garrick over the next four decades.

No matter how exercised they were over the financial security of the Garrick, it did not occur to the General Committee that admitting women members might transform the financial state of the Club – as it has done a number of gentlemen's clubs in the first years of the twenty-first century. Indeed, in the spring of 1953, they had specifically requested that ladies not be invited to dine on Thursday evenings, then, as now, still very much considered the 'Club night'. One lady who most certainly did enter the Garrick in 1957 was Ingrid Bergman, in London to appear opposite Cary Grant in the film *Indiscreet*. The Club appeared in the film as the Players, but the scenes of the pair walking up the stairs and seated in the Coffee Room pay ample tribute to how good the Club looked.

The Committee may have felt no option but to accept the fee they received for the filming because of the precariousness of the Club's finances. Certainly they were so worried that they suggested a substantial increase in membership fees – from £26.25 to £33 at an Extraordinary General Meeting in October 1958. The members turned the proposal down flat, and a special committee under the chairmanship of the respected Sebastian Earl was appointed to come up with alternative proposals. All sorts of alternatives were considered, including the introduction of fifty new members, the provision of a 'snack bar or quick lunch room', the conversion of the Morning Room into a second Coffee Room, and even the erection of a new building on the site of the Club with 'shops on the ground floor, offices above, and the top floor, including a number of bedrooms as the Club premises'. All these suggestions were however dismissed, and the members reluctantly accepted that their subscriptions would have to be increased in line with inflation.

If that annoyed them, it was nothing like the annoyance they had felt just a few months before over a member who many believed should be summarily ejected from his membership – no small matter, as he was editor of *Punch* at the time, and a noted columnist. In October 1957 Malcolm Muggeridge had asked in the American magazine *Saturday Evening Post* – 'Does England Really Need a Queen?', with its implication that the monarchy was nothing more than a club for snobs and a drain on the taxpayer. Many members of the Garrick were apoplectic with rage, calling for his immediate expulsion. One member wrote to the Chairman: 'If this person were to sit next to me in the Coffee Room, I should find it impossible to carry on the Club tradition of talking to him. It would seem other members also share my views'. Others were slightly more balanced, one commenting: 'The article you have shown me stinks, in my opinion, to high heaven ... but whether we can kick him out of the Club is another matter. I see nothing that is defamatory, though much of it is offensive at least in tone, about Prince Philip' (by then the Garrick's Patron).

On the first Thursday of November the Committee met to consider the matter, and were much influenced by a letter delivered to the recently appointed Secretary, Commander E.S. Satterthwaite, by the distinguished artist, cartoonist and writer Nicholas Bentley. 'I hold no brief for his views', Bentley wrote, 'but I should deplore any attempt to penalise him for expressing them merely because they happen to be repugnant to certain members. To deny a man the privilege of free speech is surely contrary to all the principles for which the Club stands, and I hope the Committee will consider Muggeridge's case extremely carefully before deciding to deprive him of that privilege.'

The liberal traditions of the Garrick won the day, and the Committee decided not to suggest that Muggeridge be expelled, or even to write to him suggesting that his article had been 'prejudicial to the interests of the Club'. But the rancour created by the incident was not dissipated. It rumbled on for a further seven years, until coming to a head again.

12

Blackballs

AS THE 'swinging Sixties' swept across London, and the King's Road and Carnaby Street filled with mini-skirts, Union flag jackets and scooters, so the Garrick soldiered gallantly on – but without a real spring in its step. The concept of the gentlemen's club, even one with such an artistic, even raffish history as the Garrick, seemed outdated, even doomed, in the world of Harold Wilson's 'white hot technological revolution', Mary Quant, Biba and Twiggy.

Not that the spirit within the Club itself was dimmed: not a bit of it. Lunches were booming, especially among the lawyers, who maintained the tradition of putting the court behind them for at least an hour and retiring to the Garrick for a little sustenance and good conversation, before returning to the demands of their case. It was a tradition that began to fade as the demands of the Bench and the Bar increased with the approach of the twenty-first century, but in those days judicial matters were taken at a rather more gentlemanly pace than they are today.

One notable judicial luncher was Mr Justice Melford Stevenson, who had been elected to the Club in June 1931 as a twenty-nine-year-old barrister, and was to remain one of its staunchest supporters for the next fifty-six years. Forever spoken of as Melford he was to become one of Britain's most distinguished High Court judges, and the last to be made a Privy Councillor without reaching the Court of Appeal. Flamboyant, with a pungent wit and with a taste for the spectacular, he was famous for his uninhibited descriptions of some of his own legal cases – including those of Dr Bodkin Adams, the Eastbourne poisoner ('Guilty as hell') and Ruth Ellis, the last woman to be hanged for murder in this country ('Pity she was hanged. If she had been reprieved we'd still have the death penalty').

Melford Stevenson was no less robust following his promotion to the Bench. As a young reporter on *The Times* I vividly remember his verdict on the Cambridge University students who had demonstrated against the Greek colonels in 1972 and contrived to do a great deal of damage to the Garden House Hotel in the process. He was stern, sentencing one to eighteen months and others to only marginally shorter prison terms. But that was nothing compared to what he had to say among his friends at the Garrick: 'Lot of commie layabouts', he called them, though he added that they were 'not as bad as their tutors – wish I could have put them inside'.

Melford Stevenson was certainly present at the dinner held on 6 July 1964 for the centenary of the Club's move to Garrick Street, as was another legal member, the then Chairman Viscount Bledisloe QC. Osbert Lancaster, Nicolas Bentley, Ronald Searle and John Gilroy represented the artist and cartoonist members towards the top of the centre table, while Sir Donald Wolfit represented the actors. The Club's 950 members paid forty guineas a year subscription at the time, and 50 guineas by way of a joining fee, and no less glamorous a magazine than *Queen* described the waiting list as 'two years' – calling the Garrick 'a portrait-lined Club in the heart of Theatreland, a love of which is shared by all members'. It was certainly shared by Melford Stevenson.

Although he was fond of his fellow journalist members, Melford Stevenson wasn't blind to their weaknesses, nor to the potential damage they might sometimes cause to his beloved Garrick. Indeed it might be said that if there were two teams within the Garrick as the 1960s got into full swing then Melford Stevenson was captain of the lawyers, and the BBC's fearsome interviewer and presenter Robin Day was to become captain of the journalists. On one memorable occasion when he was about to interview the then Prime Minister Harold Wilson about Labour's devaluation of the pound, Day asked Melford Stevenson: 'What should be my first question?'. There was only a moment's pause before Melford said firmly: 'Have you any idea of the meaning of the word shame?'. Both enjoyed each other's company, but there were undeniably moments when the two teams fell out.

One such moment concerned the sometimes irascible, not to say downright difficult, Malcolm Muggeridge, whose views about the British monarchy, and the Queen in particular, had caused such a stir within the Club at the end of the 1950s. The matter subsided for a time, with Muggeridge occupying his rightful place at the Garrick as a former editor of *Punch* and the latest example of that great tradition that had brought so many distinguished and enthusiastic members to the Club over the years. In spite of his membership Muggeridge's attacks on the British establishment over the years had not weakened, and as the 1960s began he had launched another, against Churchill, in the American magazine *Esquire*, which provoked a good deal of comment, but no action, among members of the Garrick.

In February 1964, however, Muggeridge took a step too far, at least in the opinion of a substantial majority of the Club's members. In an interview on American television with Jack Paar, he returned to his attack on the British monarchy and suggested, in terms that would hardly be regarded as outrageous today: 'Here are all the ingredients of a soap opera. The English are getting bored with their monarchy. I think it is coming to an end'. Only too well aware that Prince Philip, the Duke of Edinburgh, remained the Club's patron, and mindful of the Club's long links with the Crown, a group of senior members took grave exception to Muggeridge's remarks and complained to Lord Bledisloe, the Chairman, asking him to consider invoking Rule 31 of the Club rules, which allowed the General Committee to expel a member.

Another member was so incensed that he pinned a copy of a newspaper article reporting Muggeridge's interview onto the Club notice board with the note: 'Does the Committee think this is the kind of person we want to have as a member?'.

After obtaining a transcript of the American broadcast, on 5 March the General Committee unanimously dismissed the suggestion that Muggeridge should be asked to resign. But by then news of the general indignation at the Garrick had reached Muggeridge, who was still smarting from his treatment only a matter of years before. On 17 March he wrote to Commander E.S. Satterthwaite, the Secretary, asking him to 'accept my resignation as from the above date'. He added: 'For some considerable time now I have scarcely used the Club's premises, preferring the food of restaurants and company of my own choosing to that provided by the Garrick', but explaining that the catalyst had been the Club's request for a transcript of his television interview 'in order that the question of the propriety of a member of the Club speaking against the Monarchy might be considered'.

The idea alone had appalled Muggeridge, and his letter continued angrily: 'I reserve the right to say whatever I like about anything anywhere, and I have no wish to belong to a Club whose Committee might abrogate to themselves the duty of supervising in any degree my exercise of this right': Muggeridge did however ask the Secretary, in typical Garrick style, 'to convey my salutations to Barker, whose invariable consideration over the years I have greatly appreciated'. In his reply 10 April 1964 Satterthwaite told Muggeridge that the General Committee 'did not think it necessary or appropriate in the circumstances to comment further on your letter'. Inevitably, a few days later the news of his resignation, and the reasons for it, leaked out in the press and the Club was inundated with letters, both from members and outsiders, broadly supporting the decision to allow him to resign, one member regretting that 'you didn't have the guts to throw him out'.

But not every member was quite so critical of the former editor of *Punch*. Indeed one of the actor stalwarts, Robert Morley, was so disturbed by the decision that he wrote to the Secretary suggesting that Muggeridge had not been 'afforded the protection by the Committee to which, I should have thought, he was entitled', and going on to ask whether the Committee might think it advisable to 'inform the members a little more fully about this matter, telling us for instance under what rule they acted and whether there are any circumstances in which the decision can be debated at, perhaps, a General Meeting'.

It was to be the first shot across the bows in what would become a somewhat acrimonious encounter between the Committee and some of the more senior members of the Club. No sooner had the Chairman replied to Morley than the actor responded with a formal request for a Special General Meeting to discuss the issue. Naturally Morley's request was supported by some of the Club's most distinguished actor members, including Richard Attenborough, Rex Harrison, Alistair Sim and Peter Finch. But there was also support from the journalists, including Robin Day and Edward Pickering. Morley suggested that the resolution to be discussed should be 'that this Special General Meeting is gravely concerned about the circumstances which led to the resignation of Mr Malcolm Muggeridge and requests a full explanation as to what occurred'.

Not all the supporters of Morley's resolution turned out to be quite as enthusiastic as its originator had hoped. Rex Harrison wrote to explain that he hadn't been able to get into the Club and therefore felt it 'wrong of me to use my name' to call a Special General Meeting, while the Secretary's letter to Peter Finch asking him to confirm his support was returned, marked 'Gone Away'. Indeed in the end only twelve of the twenty names necessary to procure the meeting were obtained, and Morley withdrew the request – settling instead for an undertaking from the Chairman that he would answer any questions about the affair at the Annual General Meeting on 26 May 1964.

Unable to attend, Robin Day wrote to the Chairman outlining the question that worried him most about the affair, namely: 'Why was Muggeridge not informed immediately of the complaint and of the decision to obtain a transcript of his remarks?'. The matter was aired at length at the AGM and the

Chairman explained to a packed meeting that the Committee had unanimously decided that Muggeridge's conduct had not warranted his expulsion from the Club. If the Committee had considered that it might, he would have been informed, and 'given the opportunity of explaining his actions', but that had never happened – all that had happened was that the member in question had decided to resign.

Perhaps the final word on Muggeridge's departure from the Garrick is best left to the Chairman, Lord Bledisloe, who like his predecessor Lord Buckmaster, admirably summed up part of the character of the Club in a final letter to Robert Morley. 'Committees of Clubs such as the Garrick', Bledisloe wrote, 'often have difficult and delicate tasks to perform and nothing is more embarrassing than to be obliged to consider the activities of a Member in the light of Rule 31.' But, in the finest Garrick tradition, the Chairman went on to explain to Morley that not only was the Committee 'a very broad-minded body', but it was also 'alive to the fact that the Garrick Club consists of Members of every shade of political opinion and they would be very loath to operate Rule 31 except in very extreme cases'.

The camaraderie that has marked the Club throughout its history was quickly restored, to the delight of many of the ordinary members who had come to the conclusion – once even whispered by the Chairman himself – that the whole matter had become 'something of a storm in a teacup'. But then the history of the Club is littered with storms in teacups of all sorts of shapes and sizes: ask Thackeray, Dickens or Irving.

Among the storms, however, there are the more light-hearted stories. Stories of members who love the place with such a passion that they can barely bring themselves to leave after lunch or dinner, even though in the 1960s Rule 29 applied which – theoretically at least – meant that members could be fined if they remained in the Club after 11pm. It was Melford Stevenson who persuaded the 1972 Annual General Meeting to amend the rule and acknowledge what almost every member knew in any event, namely that the Garrick would remain open as long as a member wanted it to – regardless of the time of night.

These were the days before there were ten bedrooms for members' use, times when members who might have been a little bit the worse for wear at midnight were tucked up under the stairs by one of the hall porters and left to sleep there through the night while the porter locked up and went home. These were the days when Barker would 'look after' the bridge players in the evenings – for these were also the days when bridge was regularly played after dinner as well as before – and the players would urge Barker 'for just one more rubber' and the steward would look quizzically at them before agreeing to bring them another round of drinks.

These were the days when Kenneth More, star of the film version of fellow member Richard Gordon's novel *Doctor in the House* and the equally entrancing *Genevieve*, not to mention his fellow member Terence Rattigan's play *The Deep Blue Sea* was another of the Club's best loved fixtures. A member since 1954, by the beginning of the 1970s More was what one living member calls 'one of our greatest ornaments ever – a man in whose company you could simply never be miserable'. Tragically the only depiction of him in the Club is as a cameo in Gilroy's wonderful recreation of the Club's open-top bus outing to the Derby, painted in 1967, where he can be glimpsed in one corner in earnest conversation with two gypsies.

Famous for his affability, More had the habit of disappearing from time to time. On one occasion the attractions of good company, and a certain amount of alcohol, meant that he had gone missing for almost twenty-four hours, to the utter despair of his wife, actress Angela Douglas, whom he always called 'Shrimp'. When he turned up at the Club, Gerard Noel, still a member now after more than fifty years, pointed out to the man who had brought Sir Douglas Bader so memorably to the screen that he was in 'deep trouble'. Kenny (as he was always known) looked just a little sheepish.

Not long afterwards, at a meeting of one of the small clubs within the Garrick at that time known as the Burgundians, whose members included Felix Aylmer and Melford Stevenson, More was very circumspect, drinking practically nothing and deciding to leave at ten – to be sure not to subject his wife to another night of agony wondering where he was. 'Can't take any chances old darling', he told fellow member Gerard Noel as they left the Club together, 'ever since that disastrous night'. With those words ringing in their ears the two men set off to find a taxi. But they couldn't find a taxi anywhere.

Finally More spied a police car and, without a moment's hesitation, flagged it down. 'Officer I'm in terrible trouble with my wife', Kenny explained, with a very solemn expression on his face. 'I wonder. Could you possibly give me a lift home? – it's not far.' Gerard Noel stood there stunned. But the policeman was not. 'Certainly Mr More', he said. 'Hop in. And would your friend like a lift too?' The two officers duly delivered the slightly worse-for-wear Kenneth More and his friend home, with a smile. It is the perfect Garrick story, and a worthy tribute to a member who is still remembered with the most enormous affection even now, more than two decades after his death in 1982.

It was More who wrote in the second volume of his auto-biography, *More or Less*, 'I love the Garrick Club, and this has long been part of my life. If I only had enough money left in the world to pay the Club subscription and nothing else, I would pay it. I like meeting the cross section of people one finds there … you never feel stagnant there: you are plugged into life. You do not need newspapers to know what is happening or watch the news on television; there you can meet the men who make the news others read about'. Or, as he put it to Gerard Noel one day: 'You know darling, this is the best Club in the world'.

But Kenny More was certainly not the only member to love the Club in those days. The composer Sir William Walton, OM, was every bit as enthusiastic a member, although a less regular visitor after his decision to base himself on the island of Ischia in the late 1960s. Walton was immensely proud of being a member, and of the musical tradition in the Club, a tradition still symbolised by Sir Malcolm Sargent, as well as Sir Arthur Bliss, that traced its origins back to Sir Arthur Sullivan. To this day Lady Walton remembers the time she was once clearing out her husband's wardrobe, and came across a very old Garrick tie that she felt sure he would never want again and which she therefore threw into the rubbish. Several days later, she recalls still, her husband asked her, rather plaintively, where his Garrick tie was. 'Oh I threw it out', she told him, 'It was so old. You couldn't possibly have worn it'. Walton's eyes misted with tears for a moment before he told her: 'But Elgar gave it to me'.

There is something about the Garrick that inspires that kind of affection. And members also feel a strong desire to protect the Club against those who do not seem to understand it. Never was that more clearly demonstrated than in the case of Lord Chief Justice Goddard, a much-liked but controversial member who was firmly in support of capital punishment. Only nine days after Rayner Goddard's death in the early summer of 1971 a column by the writer and critic Bernard Levin appeared in *The Times* roundly condemning him for his views, even though the late Lord Chief's body had still to be interred: indeed the obituaries had only just started to appear.

Within a matter of days the Chairman, Lord Bledisloe, had received a shower of letters from members – sixty per cent of them from lawyers – complaining not so much about what was written but about the timing. Melford Stevenson was outraged, describing the column as 'scandalous muck' and insisting that it not only caused 'intense distress' to his family but also to fellow lawyers who remained members of the Club. Bledisloe admitted that the columnist had done 'something that offended many members. Their reaction was spontaneous; they were shocked'. So shocked, indeed, that when Levin's name appeared as a candidate on the notice board someone scrawled 'Never' alongside it, a gesture that was to provoke considerable speculation in the press.

By an extraordinary, some might say malevolent, coincidence, *The Times* columnist was indeed at the time a candidate for membership of the Club, and Melford vowed to stop his election, calling a meeting of the senior lawyers in the Club's Coffee Room to organise their protest. A number of the journalist members protested that one – albeit ill-timed column – should not be sufficient reason to bar an otherwise entirely suitable candidate from membership. In June 1972, however, the lawyers won. The General Committee blackballed Levin and his candidacy was rejected. His proposer, Giles Playfair, remarked ruefully afterwards that his candidate had acted 'most honourably', but that he did not know 'whether he would want to be proposed again'. In fact he never stood for membership of the Garrick again.

But the matter did not end there. Six months later twenty members demanded a Special General Meeting with a view to changing 'the way the Club Committee votes an applicant in or out of membership'. It was to be a futile gesture. More than 200 members crammed into the Coffee Room in December 1972 to consider Nicholas Bentley's motion to increase the number of blackballs necessary for a candidate to be rejected. The motion was defeated comfortably, though with more than sixty abstentions.

One member, the poet and critic Stephen Spender, was appalled, and wrote to The *Guardian* to say so: 'It is the peculiarity of Mr Levin to be opinionated, witty, vigorous and alive – and, of course, all these qualities are offensive in the eyes of certain members of clubs. But it seems extremely regrettable that on account of these blackballs the rest of us should be deprived of a member able to express controversial opinions'. He then added, 'Mr Levin is a strange mixture of sympathy and bloody-mindedness; and it is surely people like that whom one wants to meet and disagree with'.

Whether the lawyers, or the General Committee, realised it or not, the Levin blackball was to cast something of a pall over the Garrick for the next few years, some seeing the decision as spiteful and short-sighted, others thinking it should never have been allowed to happen in the first place. That single decision contrived to make the Garrick seem somehow out of tune with the times, dismissing one of the stars of the iconic 1960s BBC show *That Was The Week That Was* with a wave of its hand.

The reverberations from the Levin blackball echoed through the Club, as they had done in earlier decades. One journalist who had previously suffered such a fate in the past was the distinguished drama critic of the *Sunday Times* between the wars, James Agate, who was advised to withdraw his candidacy in 1937 for fear of a blackball. As Agate memorably put it at the time:

'Two thirds of the present membership would have blackballed Garrick'.

But blackballs were not the only reason for the difficulties that the Club encountered as it entered the 1970s. There was also the question of money – or rather the lack of it.

OH! WHAT A HUMBUG!

Amelia. "Mamma, dear! here's a Note from dear William, with a Box for the Opera, I shouldn't wonder." (Reads) :—" *My darling Amelia, Circumstances over which I have no control will take me as far as Greenwich. I find that I have left my Latch-key—please to get it from the Waistcoat I took off, and send it by the Bearer to your ever affectionate, Kiddleums.*"

13

Ladies

*B*Y THE middle of 1972, the Garrick's finances were in a parlous state, so parlous indeed that the General Committee
asked the Annual General Meeting that year to increase the
annual subscription by no less than fifty per cent: from £50 to
£75. The debate at the meeting was fierce, but, as Melford
Stevenson pointed out, 'financial reality' could hardly be avoided,
and the motion to increase the subscription was passed. As a gesture of goodwill, however, the Club agreed to abandon its
famously ignored rule that imposed fines for members that stayed
after eleven o'clock in the evening.

Aware of the need for fresh blood the General Committee
launched a campaign to try and attract younger members to add
to the vitality of the centre table, and it was at that time that a
number of the central figures among the current membership first
climbed the steps from Garrick Street. In the interests of a freer,
more relaxed atmosphere, there had also been a slight slackening
of the laws regarding the admission of women: nothing drastic, of
course, but a gentle easing.

In November 1968 it was agreed that the Secretary should
'use his discretion in permitting ladies to enter the Club in the

evening wearing trousers'. With the slightest trace of tongue in cheek, the General Committee ruled that as the guiding principle 'a lady who had obviously gone home and changed for the occasion should certainly be admitted'. And in December 1971 women were welcomed into the Cocktail Bar — which had recently moved from what is now the Reading Room at the top of the stairs into its current position — but only on Sunday evenings, hardly the busiest night of the week in the Club.

Nevertheless by 1976 there came a major breakthrough in the creation of a Ladies Cloakroom in the Club, and the recognition that women could be entertained in what had become known as the Milne Room, the large private room on the right at the top of the stairs from the Porter's Lodge, which some of the older members could still recall as a retiring room where they could sleep in the afternoons. The following year they were also to be welcomed in the Morning Room before lunch, and in October 1979 they won the grand accolade: ladies were now allowed to use the main staircase at any time, having until then been condemned to the side stairs to the right of the entrance from the street. Female guests seemed to enjoy the experience. The *Observer*'s columnist, Katherine Whitehorn, noted shortly after the changes: 'The Garrick girl is great — she is temperamental and ebullient: her powder room has theatrical prints, a statue of a bare-breasted nymph beating another on the bottom with a hairbrush, sal volatile and a chaise-longue on which La Duse would have been proud to have the vapours'.

The traditions of the Garrick were not to be dismissed lightly when it came to 'girls' however, and Thursday evenings, always known as 'Club night', were sacrosanct for many years after women were admitted — indeed members were firmly reminded that ladies were not welcome in the Coffee Room as guests on that particular night of the week. In fact they were not even welcome in a private dining room on that evening, as Arthur Crook, a former editor of the *Times Literary Supplement* and still a member, vividly recalls.

Crook's predecessor as editor of the *TLS* Alan Pryce-Jones had organised a small dinner party in a private room for a number

of guests, including the poet Edmund Blunden, the authoress
Rose Macaulay and the Duchess of Buccleuch. The dinner began
pleasantly enough, but then Satters, the Secretary, looked in and
said to Pryce-Jones, rather fiercely: 'You realise what day of the
week it is?'. The host murmured 'Thursday' fairly meekly, and
Satters barked back: 'No ladies allowed in the Club on a
Thursday', before adding rapidly, in a wonderfully Garrick compromise, 'Well, we can't do anything now, it's too late.
Everybody's in here, but can I ask you?'. After a pause, he continued: 'Can I ask your two ladies that if, for any reason, they
have to leave the room and bump into members, if they're asked
what they're doing, they explain that they work here?'. As Crook
recalled recently: 'So the Duchess and Rose Macaulay were honorary cleaners or something'. The rule prohibiting lady guests on
Thursday evenings was not revoked until 1978.

One 'Garrick Girl' who was fêted by the Club was Dame
Anna Neagle. By 27 March 1971 she had notched up 2,047 performances in the musical *Charlie Girl*, an all-time record for an
actress in the history of British theatre, and a lunch was duly
given in her honour, with Kenneth More in the chair. Other
guests included Dame Sybil Thorndike, Alec Guinness and Basil
Dean. Barely three months later there was another lunch for a
Garrick Girl, this time Marie Löhr, who had presented the Club
with eight silver plates originally given to Sir Beerbohm Tree by
the cast of *Henry V* at Christmas 1910. This lunch was given by
Sir John Gielgud, Andrew Cruickshank, Roland Culver, David
Langton and Donald Sinden to celebrate her gift.

In these more difficult times the actors seemed to come to
the fore at the Club. The annual dinner in 1971 was to honour
Sir John Gielgud's fifty years in the theatre, and he, together with
John Clements, Alistair Sim, Jack Hawkins, Nöel Coward, Alec
Guinness, Laurence Olivier and many many others seemed to
give the Club a sparkle, no matter how dire the financial circumstances behind the scenes may have been. One member at
the time vividly recalls lunching with Wolfit and Michael
Redgrave, when they started to discuss playing Hamlet. 'I was all
agog', he was to write afterwards, 'but their talk was all about the

absolute hell of playing Hamlet at matinees and "all those bloody tea trays"'.

Wolfit's appetite for the Garrick knew few bounds, as Ronald Harwood, an enthusiastic member still, and at one point the great man's dresser, before becoming a playwright, often recalls. One story, in particular, captures Wolfit's delight in the Club and its traditions. He was giving lunch at a side table to an ambitious young actor anxious to join his theatre company, and asking him about his interest in Shakespeare and what parts he might like to play. Everything was going swimmingly, when Wolfit said suddenly: 'Right, come with me, my boy', put down his knife and fork, in the middle of the main course, got up from his chair and marched out of the Coffee Room, dragging the young actor in his wake. The two men went through the door, down the steps and into the street. When they got outside, Wolfit turned to his puzzled guest and announced: 'The salary will be £2.50 a week. Is that all right for you?'. The young man muttered: 'Yes, Sir. Thank you very much Sir'. And they walked back into the Club, sat down and finished their lunch. Wolfit was only too well aware of the Garrick rule that no business shall be discussed inside the Club.

The chef at the time was the remarkable cockney Leonard Coleman, a teetotaller and non-smoker, whose best-loved dish among the members was jugged hare. In those days the members preferred what would now be called 'nursery food' – sausages and mash, steak and kidney pie, after which some members still hanker, rather than the more elaborate 'restaurant' dishes that have tended to replace them in recent years. But the Garrick, in common with other London clubs, acknowledged that it had to change with the times. Nowhere was that more abundantly clear than with the decision in November 1972 of the estimable 'Satters', Commander Satterthwaite, the Secretary, to resign after two decades in the post – to be replaced not long afterwards by the current incumbent, Martin Harvey, still there after three decades. 'I still miss Satters', one current member confessed recently, 'It was the way he used to sway after lunch, as if he was still on the bridge of a destroyer: utterly unforgettable. He never ever seemed to go home'.

Sadly the 1970s also brought with them a number of deaths. Indeed many of the great characters, some of the flower of the Garrick during the first half of the twentieth century, died within a few months of each other. Satters's predecessor Colonel S.E. Baddeley died in 1971, and Jack Hawkins and John Clements followed within a year or two, as did Sir Nöel Coward and Sir Robin Darwin, former principal of the Royal College of Art, not to mention G.O. 'Gully' Nickalls, Olympic oarsman and a member of the Club since 1929, and Sir Julian Hall, theatrical critic and novelist, member since 1928 and a Trustee to boot. The American movie star John Wayne fell in love with the Club while in London making the film *Brannigan*: 'I would just love to settle in there and read their 5,000 books on the theatre', he is reported to have said, 'I'd rather do that than ride horses'. But such sentiments couldn't disguise the fact that the Club was changing.

By great good fortune, however, just as some of the Garrick's most distinguished members began to disappear and their survivors sink into a despair, so the Club's fortunes took a turn for the better – thanks to the generosity of one of its former writer members, and the indelible popularity of one of his creations, Winnie-the-Pooh. Alan Alexander Milne, playwright, detective novelist, and writer of children's stories, had died in 1956, leaving a portion of his estate to the Club – even though there is no record of this quiet, reserved man ever playing a particularly active role in the Club during his almost forty years of membership.

The first signs of just how valuable Milne's bequest would be did not begin to surface, however, until the end of the 1970s – condemning the members to struggle throughout the decade with rapidly increasing annual subscriptions, and a need to bump up the membership as speedily as possible to keep the balance sheet suitably afloat. In 1975, for example, the annual subscription had risen again to £108, causing a substantial defection among the members, though not as large as that reported in the press. Neither Alec Guinness nor Michael Redgrave, for example, chose to resign, despite the contrary being widely reported. And another member of the time, the Tory politician Reginald

Maudling, chose instead to resign from the Carlton rather than the Garrick.

Over the next decade a steady, and ever-increasing, flow of royalties from the stories, the films and the marketing of Milne's characters, Pooh, Eeyore and Christopher Robin, would contrive to solve the Club's financial difficulties — while, at the same time, the number of candidates for membership expanded rapidly. Indeed in the past five years Milne's legacy has secured the Club's existence, and financial security, into the foreseeable future — providing its investments are handled wisely. In 2000 the Disney Corporation offered the Club a capital sum in exchange for the annual royalties it was paying to the Garrick, and the other beneficiaries of Milne's estate. This brought the Club a windfall of approaching £40m before tax, a great deal of which is now invested to secure the Club's future into its second century.

The possibility of such good fortune seemed a long way off in the dark days of the mid-1970s, when the Club could not even afford to refurbish. That sense of gloom may have accounted for one or two other notable moments of bad temper over blackballs — all of them directed, as usual, against journalists aspiring to become members. Anthony Howard, then editor of the *New Statesman*, suffered just such an indignity but, unlike Levin, rapidly overcame the hiccough and went on to become a loyal member. But the fact that the Garrick received £32,000 in royalties from the Milne estate in 1976 helped to lighten the mood.

Meanwhile the Club's leading lights from the post-war years continued to be snuffed out. 1978 saw the loss of Basil Dean, founder of ENSA and producer extraordinaire, a member since 1939, as well as Sir Terence Rattigan, a member since 1944 and the Garrick's premier playwright of the time, who just outgunned fellow playwright member Freddie Lonsdale. The following year saw the death of the Club's former Chairman, Lord Bledisloe, who had coped with the Muggeridge and many other affairs. But none of these departures contrived to mute the ever jovial spirit of the Club. As current member Alan Watkins so memorably reported at the time: 'You can always tell when the Garrick is shut because you can hear people laughing in the bar of the Travellers'. The two clubs had reciprocal holiday arrangements during their summer closures, as most do.

No one could have captured that slightly mischievous Garrick spirit better than Laurence Olivier, by then in his seventies. Due to appear on the stage later that evening, the director of the National Theatre was sharing an early supper at the head of the centre table with one or two of his fellow actors when the Secretary's secretary arrived to show some American ladies, art lovers all, the finest of the Club's paintings: 'And these are the Zoffanys', she announced, as she ushered the visitors into the Coffee Room and waved to the wall to the left of the door. Olivier immediately rose to his feet, so legend has it, gave a courtly bow to the ladies, and said, without a moment's pause: 'I am Poppa Zoffany, and these are my boys Rocco, Giovanni ...'. In another version of that same story, one of the American ladies is said to have whispered to the Secretary's secretary as she made her announcement: 'Oh, don't disturb them, they're having their supper'.

By the end of the decade the Garrick was back on its feet: the Milne bequest easing its finances, the Coffee Room packed both at lunch and dinner, and the waiting list for membership extended to almost four years. The Club has barely looked back since, for the 1980s cemented the success. At that time it was still open at weekends for lunch – braised ox tongue and spinach was £2.20 in the far-off days of 1980, while half a carafe of Club wine cost £1.70.

In September 1981 the Garrick celebrated the 150th anniversary of its foundation with a Service of Thanksgiving and Dedication at St Paul's Covent Garden, just round the corner, and always the Club's favourite church, in spite of the somewhat dubious acoustics that infuriate the older members whose hearing may not be quite as good as it once was. Nevertheless, all those present could hear each and every syllable of Sir John Gielgud's reading. As they could William Douglas-Home's speech at a celebratory dinner at the Club two months later which was attended by the Club's patron the Duke of Edinburgh. The leather-bound book containing the signatures of everyone there that evening remains in the Library.

As it had done over the previous eight generations, subtly, but irrevocably, the order was changing again at the Garrick. It is impossible to say exactly when this happens, but no member can mistake it when it does. The great beasts of a former generation slip gently away, to be replaced by the next generation who come to leave their signature on the Club. In the wake of Kenneth More, whose death in 1982 was mourned by every member, came Donald Sinden, a member since 1960, who took his place as one of the Club's leading actors, and a Trustee – a position that More had turned down because of the onset of Parkinson's disease. Meanwhile, the ever-present Raymond Huntley, portrayer on screen of a generation of bank managers and unhappy fathers, glared down the centre table at lunchtimes, an enthusiastic if never exactly cheerful actor member whose presence cast a spell over the 1980s.

The journalists may have been the subject of occasional blackballs, but their contribution to the Garrick was strongly represented in the 1980s by Robin Day, who had arrived in 1963, William Rees-Mogg, now Lord Rees-Mogg, who had become a member two years later, and Peregrine Worsthorne of the *Sunday Telegraph*, who had followed them in 1971, arriving as a member just two years before the man who would come to symbolise the Club in the last years of the twentieth century – Kingsley Amis. If there was one great beast of the jungle in the Garrick as the 1990s began, it was undoubtedly Kingsley – his presence seemed to dominate the Cocktail Bar and overshadow almost every other member, with the exceptions of Sir John Gielgud and Sir Alec Guinness, neither of whom came as frequently as he did, and certainly not Laurence Olivier, whose death in 1989 marked the passing of another era. Only the lawyer, and later Attorney General and Lord Chancellor Michael Havers, father of the actor Nigel, renowned for his penchant for the occasional political indiscretion in the Club, ran Kingsley anything like a close second.

It was Kingsley, together with actor William Fox and Roger Morgan, son of the distinguished critic, playwright and novelist Charles Morgan, one of the jewels of the Garrick in the 1930s, who founded one of the more extraordinary 'clubs within the Club' one Friday afternoon in the 1980s. Never a man to be rushed down to lunch, Kingsley – who maintained that the five worst words in the English language were 'Shall we go straight in?' (to lunch that is) – was enjoying himself in the Bar along with a number of fellow members, including Fox and Morgan. As two o'clock approached, the suggestion was made that perhaps they should go down to lunch, but it was another ten minutes or so before they actually did so. When they finally arrived at the Coffee Room the motley members found it was full – and were pointed to the private dining room opposite. They enjoyed themselves so much – not least because they could be even noisier than they could in the Coffee Room – that they founded the '1400' club to commemorate the fact that they would not sit down to eat before two o'clock. Indeed they still meet on the first Friday of every month to this day, though the membership has changed as the years have passed.

The Garrick thrived as the century came to an end. The waiting list extended to six and then seven years, even though the membership had expanded to 1,100; the Milne royalties provided it with a substantial cheque from the Disney Corporation twice a year, until a final capital sum of almost £40m before the payment of tax was agreed in 2001; and a programme of refurbishment began to smarten up an interior that had become a little shabby. Others preferred the shabbiness. But the Garrick would not be the Garrick without a disagreement or two.

One disagreement even spilled out into what was then the Royalty (now the Peacock) Theatre in nearby Kingsway in 1992, when the issue of lady members was formally raised for the first time in the Club's history at a Special General Meeting. Held in a theatre to accommodate all the members, the meeting was heated, but never angry, and decided by an overwhelming majority not to admit women as members. There were one or two unhappy members as a result, including one leading human rights lawyer who resigned 'in protest' (although not until three years later), but the majority felt, as one put it at the meeting, 'We could not be more welcoming to lady guests than we are – I just think lady members would change the place beyond words'. Most members never want the Garrick to change. As the *Observer* commented the day before the vote on lady members: 'The worst you can say with certainty about the Garrick is that some people find its particular brand of bufferishnesss fairly tedious. Its members, however, think it the best club in London – and their guests are inclined to agree'.

Nowhere is the bonhomie that lies at the very heart of the Garrick better expressed than in John Gilroy's painting of the Club's outing to the Derby in June 1967. Now sadly tucked away on the rear stairs Gilroy's sprightly picture shows the legendary Barker dancing a jig in front of the two open-top buses that transported the members to Epsom Downs. Among the fifty-eight members and friends depicted are Robin Day, actor Nigel Patrick, Pat Kirkwood and Hubert Gregg, Michael Havers and Kenneth More. A sense of sheer fun shines out of the painting.

By the early 1990s the members were certainly every bit as diverse a bunch as their predecessors had been a century and a half before. Politicians were represented, as were playwrights, television personalities, publishers and, of course, lawyers. Among those serving on the Garrick committees, for example, the law was represented by Michael Davies, Anthony Butcher and Charles Potter; while the media included Michael Charlton, Tom Pocock, Arthur Crook, Brian Masters and Peregrine Worsthorne. But the actors were not to be outshone. Many of them have served on the Club's committees, including, for example, Geoffrey Palmer, Ian Wallace, Peter Sallis, Frederick Treves and, of course, Donald Sinden, who was a Trustee for many years.

But it was still, somehow, the lawyers and the journalists who seemed to spar at the centre of the Garrick's life. It was a journalist who was to become another prominent casualty of the Garrick's occasional appetite for a public blackballing that was to cause the only controversy of the final years of the twentieth century. In a decision that his proposer rightly described as 'perverse', in November 1993 the General Committee decided that the television interviewer and author Jeremy Paxman should not be elected to membership. It was hardly the Club's finest hour – not least for an institution that counted another, perhaps even more famous television inquisitor, Robin Day, among its membership – bringing back memories of Melford Stevenson's remark, towards the end of his life, about Bernard Levin: 'If someone put the chap up now, I shouldn't object'.

Indeed it was the Club's individualist streak that saw the members firmly eschew individual financial handouts as a result of the Disney Corporation's offer to buy out the remaining years of the Milne royalties with a capital sum. At another meeting at a nearby theatre – the Fortune this time – in August 1998 the members agreed to secure the financial future of the Club itself, and set up a charitable trust, rather than each take some £40,000 as a result of the deal, which would eventually bring the Club a little under £30m after tax. Almost everyone there that day felt that this was the greatest gift the current members could give to their successors – the certainty that the Garrick would continue to exist.

One manifestation of the Garrick's windfall was a prize for artists. Determined to keep the art of theatrical portraiture alive, the Club initiated a three-yearly Garrick Milne Prize in 2000 for artists working in the field. The winner, who receives a cheque for £20,000, sees his or her painting hang first in the Club itself, and then in a West End theatre for a time, the aim being to encourage artists to capture actors and performers during rehearsal or performance. Another innovation was a quarterly newsletter, *The Garrick*.

When the cheque from Disney had finally been cashed, after some lengthy negotiations, in 2001 the Garrick celebrated in true Club style by throwing what its Chairman, the distinguished barrister Anthony Butcher QC, called a 'beano' at the home of the Honourable Artillery Company in the City of London. The sight of some of the country's leading barristers crashing wholeheartedly into one another on the dodgem cars demanded the talents of Gilroy – who, sadly, was no longer at hand.

DELICATE TEST.

Elevated Party. "A NEVER THINK A FL'ER'S HAD T'MUSH WINE S'LONG AS A WINDSUP-ISH WASH!"   *[Proceeds to perform that operation with corkscrew.*

~ 14 ~

Under the Stairs

I F THE Garrick has a heart, it is under the stairs in the entrance hall. It is here that the General Committee tends to gather before its meetings early on Thursday evenings, here that the members sometimes congregate before lunch, and retire to after lunch or dinner, and here that the candidates' books and the suggestion book are to be found. Unlikely though it may seem, these few ancient leather chairs in front of the fire, surrounded by maroon curtains, and standing on a carpet that has seen better days, represent the very essence of the Club, even in the twenty-first century.

If the Garrick is the Holy of Holies of the chattering classes, as more than one member has described it in the public prints, then under the stairs is its high altar – prohibited to non-members until after seven in the evening, and to ladies at any time, although legend has it that the rule was waived for the late Queen Elizabeth the Queen Mother. It is under the stairs that the Club is at its truest, its most relaxed, and its most refreshing; here that the warmth that so many members describe is most clearly in evidence, and that has not changed at all as the years have passed. The Club may occasionally be refurbished, made to look a little grander, but there is an element of shabby down-at-heel gentility under the stairs that somehow represents its very soul.

No one can hide under the stairs. Visitors and members alike can see, and hear, what is going on here. It is a small stage, but a central one to the Club's tradition, a reflection of its trait of self-display, where every member seems almost to regard every other as a star of some kind or other. There is the atmosphere of the Green Room about it, gossipy, supportive but distinctly theatrical — a firm reflection of the Club's origins and its ambitions. It's not for nothing that the salmon-and-cucumber tie takes a certain courage to wear in public, nor that under the stairs is so open for all to see, for there is an element of exhibitionism among every member of the Garrick.

It is here too that the members seem closest to the staff. Not only Maura Egan, Carlo Forte and Francesco D'Ambros who stand guard outside their beloved Coffee Room — which Maura for one has watched over with a motherly eye for longer than any of her members care to remember — but also the other waiters, waitresses and wine waiters — like the incomparable and only recently-retired Peter Ellick — who ebb and flow on their way to and from the other rooms. There aren't really any backstairs to the Garrick, no green baize door to hide the staff from the members — the Club is too democratic for that. Every member cherishes the staff every bit as much as they do fellow members, for remembering them, making them feel welcome, and reminding them that they are part of an institution with roots that stretch back to the London of William IV. Under the stairs is the Piccadilly Circus of the Garrick — stand or sit there long enough and you will meet everyone, and anyone, you want to.

But if under the stairs is the heart of the Club then the Cocktail Bar is its lungs. Now presided over by Harry Soekarni, who took over from the still lamented Tony Wilde in 1996, together with John Croke, it houses the best of the Garrick's more contemporary portraits of actors, including Allan Aynesworth and Lewis Casson, Laurence Olivier and Alec Guinness, Peter Ustinov and Alistair Sim, not to mention an extraordinarily young-looking Donald Sinden and a marvellous portrait of Constance

Cummings as a young woman. But it isn't so much the art that
is striking as the noise. The Garrick's bar has always been famous
for its animation, particularly on Thursday evenings, which are
still regarded as Club nights, and on many a Friday lunchtime,
particularly when the 1400 Club are meeting.

There is a level of jollity and cheer in the bar that is to be
found in few other London clubs, perhaps a reflection of the
Garrick's origin as a meeting place for those of more dubious
social standing. No one, be they a former Chancellor of the
Exchequer, Lord Chief Justice, star of a long-running television
series, author of that week's best-seller, chief executive of a super-
market, or agent to the world's most famous footballer, is viewed
as anything other than a member. There is no edge, no awareness of position, no care with protocol, for that is not what the
Garrick is about. There is only good fellowship – no matter how
old-fashioned that may sound – and, perhaps significantly, ladies
are not allowed across the threshold until 9pm.

It was in the Bar that the late Kingsley Amis held court,
sitting in his favourite chair in front of the right-hand sash window, and regaling his fellow members with wonderful stories. His
poem in praise of the Bar remains framed in the farthest corner.
No one could have captured its charms more accurately.

> Look at old Morrison!
> Isn't he wonderful?
> Fit as a fiddle
>   And tight as a tick;
>
> Seventy-seven
> And spouting his stories –
> Just listen a minute
>   And laugh yourself sick.
>
> Same with the other chaps,
> Bloody good company,
> Never let anyone
>   Drink on his own;

Out of your parish
Or widowed or derelict,
Once you're in here
      You're never alone.

Different for Wetherby,
Stuck with incontinence,
Mute in his wheelchair
      And ready to go;

Different for Hooper,
Put back on the oxygen,
Breathing, but breathing
      Uncommonly slow.

Did what we could, of course,
While there was anything,
Best to remember 'em
      Not as they are,

But as they used to be —
Chattering, chaffing, and ...
You go and eat
      And I'll stay in the bar.

There could be no finer evocation of the spirit of the Bar, although it no longer serves the Gin Punch for which it was once rightly famous, indeed firmly recommended by Phiz, the illustrator of Dickens. 'Try that Gin Punch' he would say 'and then see'. The recipe survives: 'Pour half a pint of gin on to the outer peel of a lemon; add the lemon juice, sugar, a little marschino, a pint and a quarter of water, and two bottles of soda water'. Legend has it that one of the founder members, Theodore Hook, on one occasion took six glasses of this 'with the accompaniment of one or two mutton chops and only stopped lest he should be late for dinner at Lord Canterbury's'.

Nowadays a member might be more tempted to slip away after quite so much punch to the quiet isolation of the Pinero Room tucked away on the rear stairs for a gentle snooze, much as he might have done before the war in the Smoking Room, which has now become the Milne Room to the right of the entrance stairs. The Pinero Room is an offshoot of one of the Garrick's best-kept secrets, the Library. A true jewel in its crown, the Library on the second floor, presided over by the fastidious and supremely informed Enid Foster, can rightly claim to be one of the finest theatrical collections in the world, with an extraordinary collection of first editions, plays, manuscripts and playbills.

The Library also possesses a collection of Charles Mathews mezzotints and the twenty-two volumes devoted to Irving himself by his biographer, and the Club's first historian, Percy Fitzgerald. There are prompt copies prepared for Covent Garden by John Philip Kemble and an exceptional assemblage of early nineteenth-century titles. But the gems are not all of quite that vintage. There is also the manuscript of James Barrie's *The Will* and the typescript of Harley Granville Barker's *The Voysey Inheritance*, not to mention a vast collection of material presented by Pinero himself.

There were moments in the 1960s and early 1970s when hard times for the Club meant that its entire existence came under threat and the sale of the whole collection had to be considered. Fortunately, through the efforts of the then chairman of the Library Committee, Sir Julian Hall, only a part was sold and the rest was thoroughly reorganised. Details of the entire collection will soon be available on the Garrick's website, a terminal for which sits silently in the Pinero Room waiting to be examined by members.

On the second floor beside the Library stands the Billiard Room, a touch neglected as the years have passed, but still graced by Henry O'Neill's portrait of forty-three members playing a game of pool in 1869 – perhaps most notorious for the white-bearded gentleman wearing a striped shirt with his left hand on the table, just to the right of Henry King, who is actually playing a shot. The tall gentleman is, of course, James Robertson Anderson, the man who blackballed Irving. But if you look at the picture carefully you will also find Trollope (on the left at the back), Lord Leighton (in the centre just over Anderson's left shoulder) and Millais (on the right-hand side with a cue in hand and a rapt expression on his face).

Billiards and pool were the only games played at the Garrick for many years — indeed it was the 1970s before snooker made an appearance in the Club — but that did nothing to dampen the enthusiasm of the player members, of which the author of *Gamesmanship*, Stephen Potter, was one, and Arthur Ransome another.

On the same floor as the Library and Billiard Room lie four of the Garrick's new bedrooms — the remaining six are on the third floor still — and the view of Nelson's Column is well worth making the climb for. Not created until the 1990s, the bedrooms have become one of the Club's most desirable features — much admired by members and reciprocal members alike, not least since they have almost all now been improved with the addition of air conditioning, though you will not find a television set in one of them. A radio is all the Club feels a visiting member might need by way of entertainment — as there is a television set in the Reading Room beside the Cocktail Bar, if one is clever enough to be able to understand its technology.

The addition of bedrooms meant that the Club had to be staffed throughout the week, and weekend, though full weekend opening is now a thing of the past. But it is possible for members and their guests to have breakfast in the Garrick on Saturday and Sunday mornings, even if you are not staying. It is served in the Irving Room, and very fine it is too, with kippers and smoked salmon, scrambled eggs and the rest of the traditional English breakfast on offer, along with half bottles of champagne, if the previous evening has been a particularly testing one. At lunchtime the Irving Room accommodates members who wish to bring lady guests, and after 9.30 in the evening undergoes its final transformation into the Grill Room providing after-theatre suppers to members and their guests, presided over by the ever cheerful Gerry Peruzzo. The Secretary declares that the Grill too will stay open 'as late as the members want it to', though common sense dictates that by 1am things are beginning to draw to a close.

'The Garrick does not close until the last member has gone home' is the rule, and so it remains. 'If a member wants to retire under the stairs for a time he is quite entitled to', insists the Secretary. In the days before the Garrick had bedrooms there were evenings when elderly members were tucked up there in blankets by the hall porter if it had grown too late for them to risk the journey home – and the porter would lock the door behind him when he left. Now, of course, there is a porter on duty throughout the night, and the members don't seem to take quite as much advantage of that facility as once they did. Now there is the mystery 'Chairman's bedroom', situated in what was once the Secretary's office, which may be available to see them through what would otherwise be a long night.

A reluctance to leave is one of the characteristics of a Garrick member. 'Like a honeypot', as more than one member has said over the years. 'I never want to go home', say many others – sometimes to the consternation of their wives and loved ones – though by no means always. Eighty years ago the Club's benefactor A.A. Milne told an interviewer that his wife encouraged him 'to go to my Club every day: she said that it brightens me up and that I bring back plenty of good stories'. It was a remark that underlines some, but not all, of the charms of what its members maintain is the finest club in London.

The Garrick today is the creation of its two most recent chairmen, the late Nunc Willcox, who sadly died only recently, and who chaired the Club for a dozen years until 1995, and his successor, Anthony Butcher QC, who took over the role and remained in the post until 2002. Between them they ushered the Garrick into the twenty-first century with diplomacy and skill. For one thing is certain – the members seldom agree about anything, and gently to guide them towards decisions demands a subtlety of touch that few possess.

As you walk across the entrance hall to this day you feel there is something unmistakable in the air – a sense of history, an awareness of the other members who have walked this way before you. If you set out up the stairs to the Cocktail Bar you pass a framed copy of Irving's candidate's page, not to mention a letter from Trollope to Browning inviting him to dine at the Club — with a postscript explaining that B. fell ill and died a few weeks later. Every step you take is somehow in the steps of history — and yet there is also a distinctly contemporary atmosphere to match it: with news of the latest first night, political intrigue, judicial decision and media conflagration.

For the Garrick renews itself constantly, with contemporary actors arriving to supplement Donald Sinden and Henry McGee, both Trustees in their time, and replace too the past giants of stage and screen; then there is the current Lord Chief Justice following his predecessors on the Bench, the last editor of *The Times*, the current editors of the *Guardian*, the *Sunday Telegraph* and the *Daily Mail* standing in for their newspaper predecessors, and the Bishop of London representing the Church. There are also still a steady number of politicians, among them Kenneth Clarke, the Lords Carlisle, Parkinson and Hattersley to represent that other 'best club in London', the Houses of Parliament.

But the Garrick is not about any individual's achievement, no matter how great that may be. It is about good fellowship among its members, for it is they who give the Club its unique atmosphere. The ghosts encourage them.

∽ *Bibliography* ∼

C.K. Adams, A Catalogue of the Pictures in the Garrick Club, (Garrick Club, London, 1936).

Geoffrey Ashton (Kalman A. Burnim & Andrew Wilton, eds.), *Pictures in the Garrick Club: A Catalogue of the paintings, drawings, watercolours and sculpture*, (Garrick Club, London, 1997).

Rev. R.H. Barham, *The Garrick Club: Notices of One Hundred and Thirty-five of its Former Members*, (printed privately, London, 1896).

Madeleine Bingham, *Henry Irving and The Victorian Theatre*, (George Allen & Unwin, London, 1978).

Guy Boas, *The Garrick Club 1831-1947*, (Garrick Club, London, 1948).

Guy Boas, *The Garrick Club 1831-1964*, (Garrick Club, London, 1964).

Kalman A. Burnim & John Baskett, *Brief Lives: Sitters and Artists in the Garrick Club Collection*, (Garrick Club, London, 2003).

Kalman A. Burnim & Andrew Wilton, *The Richard Bebb Collection in the Garrick Club: A Catalogue of Figures, Sculpture and Paintings*, (Unicorn Press, London, 2001).

T.H.S. Escott, *Club Makers and Club Members*, (T. Fisher Unwin, London, 1914).

Percy Fitzgerald, F.S.A., *The Garrick Club*, (Elliot Stock, London, 1904).

Tom Girtin, *The Abominable Clubman*, (Hutchinson & Co. Ltd., London, 1964).

Joseph Hatton, *Club-Land: London and Provincial*, (J.S. Virtue & Co. Ltd., London, 1890).

Richard Hough, *The Ace of Clubs: A History of the Garrick*, (Andre Deutsch, London, 1986).

Laurence Irving, *Henry Irving: The Actor and His World*, (Faber & Faber, London, 1951).

Edgar Johnson, *Charles Dickens: His Tragedy and Triumph*, (Victor Gollancz Ltd., London, 1953), Vols. I & II.

Ian McIntyre, *Garrick*, (Allen Lane, The Penguin Press, London, 1999).

Graham Reynolds et al., *Charles Dickens* (exh.cat., Victoria & Albert Museum, London, 1970).

George Winchester Stone, Jr. & George M. Kahrl, *David Garrick: A Critical Biography*, (Southern Illinois University Press, 1979).

Ann Thwaite, *A.A. Milne: His Life*, (Faber & Faber, London, 1990).

John Timbs, F.S.A., *Club Life of London with Anecdotes of the Clubs, Coffee-Houses and Taverns of the Metropolis during the 17th, 18th, and 19th Centuries*, (Richard Bentley, London, 1866), Vol.I.

J.C. Trewin (ed.), *The Journal of William Charles Macready*, (Longmans, Green & Co., London, 1967).

Robert Walters, *Catalogue of the Pictures and Miniatures in the possession of the Garrick Club*, (Eyre & Spottiswoode, London, 1909).

Mary Webster, *Johan Zoffany 1733-1810*, (National Portrait Gallery, London, 1976).

~ *Index* ~